101 WAYS TO MAKE STUDYING EASIER AND FASTER FOR COLLEGE STUDENTS

WHAT EVERY STUDENT NEEDS TO KNOW EXPLAINED SIMPLY

REVISED 2ND EDITION

Susan M. Roubidoux & Lindsey Carman

101 WAYS TO MAKE STUDYING EASIER AND FASTER FOR COLLEGE STUDENTS: WHAT EVERY STUDENT NEEDS TO KNOW EXPLAINED SIMPLY REVISED 2ND EDITION

Copyright © 2015 Atlantic Publishing Group, Inc.
1405 SW 6th Avenue • Ocala, Florida 34471 • Phone 800-814-1132 • Fax 352-622-1875
Web site: www.atlantic-pub.com • E-mail: sales@atlantic-pub.com
SAN Number: 268-1250

Library of Congress Cataloging-in-Publication Data

Roubidoux, Susan Marie, 1976-
  101 ways to make studying easier and faster for college students : what every student needs to know explained simply / by Susan M. Roubidoux. -- Revised Second edition.
    pages cm
  Includes bibliographical references and index.
  ISBN 978-1-60138-944-2 (alk. paper) -- ISBN 1-60138-944-2 (alk. paper) 1. Study skills--United States. 2. College student orientation--United States. 3. Active learning--United States. I. Title. II. Title: One hundred one ways to make studying easier and faster for college students.
  LB2395.R76 2015
  371.30281--dc23
                    2014033741

2ND EDITION EDITOR: Melissa Shortman • mfigueroa@atlantic-pub.com
INTERIOR LAYOUT: Antoinette D'Amore • addesign@videotron.ca
COVER DESIGN: Meg Buchner • megadesn@mchsi.com

Printed in the United States

Printed on Recycled Paper

Reduce. Reuse.
RECYCLE.

A decade ago, Atlantic Publishing signed the Green Press Initiative. These guidelines promote environmentally friendly practices, such as using recycled stock and vegetable-based inks, avoiding waste, choosing energy-efficient resources, and promoting a no-pulping policy. We now use 100-percent recycled stock on all our books. The results: in one year, switching to post-consumer recycled stock saved 24 mature trees, 5,000 gallons of water, the equivalent of the total energy used for one home in a year, and the equivalent of the greenhouse gases from one car driven for a year.

Over the years, we have adopted a number of dogs from rescues and shelters. First there was Bear and after he passed, Ginger and Scout. Now, we have Kira, another rescue. They have brought immense joy and love not just into our lives, but into the lives of all who met them.

We want you to know a portion of the profits of this book will be donated in Bear, Ginger and Scout's memory to local animal shelters, parks, conservation organizations, and other individuals and nonprofit organizations in need of assistance.

*– **Douglas & Sherri Brown,***
*****President & Vice-President of Atlantic Publishing*****

DEDICATION

To Doug:
Because of you, I am able to follow my heart
and be the person I wanted to be.
I love you.

To Mom and Dad:
Thank you for giving me the love of reading,
language and learning.

To Teri, Adrienne, and Emily:
The memories of our college friendship
have made writing this book so entertaining.

TABLE OF CONTENTS

Preface..**11**

Introduction...**13**
    Obstacles That College Students Battle 14
    Characteristics of Successful College Students 16
    How to Use This Book.. 17

PART I : Setting Yourself Up for Success: What to Do Right Now **19**

Chapter 1: Make a Schedule **21**
    Determine Where Time Goes... 22
    Determine the Best Study Time 23
    Set Up a Regular Schedule. 24
    Commit to Going to Each and Every Class Meeting 26
    Plan Study Blocks 27
    Compensate for Special Circumstances 28
    Make Time for Fun... 29
    Make Use Of Your Breaks 31
    Survive Those Crazy Weeks 32
    Exercise: Create a Schedule 33
    Have Multiple Spots 41

Chapter 2: Find a Study Spot **41**
    Know Which Spots to Avoid 42
    Know Where to Look.. 43
    Keep a Secret 43
    Exercise: Find and Evaluate Potential Secret Study Spots 44
    Exercise: Plan Where You Will Study at Each Study Session........... 46
    Organize the Backpack... 47

Chapter 3: Get Organized **47**
   Organize the Papers.. 48
   Dress for Success 49
   Exercise: Organize Study Supplies 50
   Exercise: Organize Class Materials... 51
   Exercise: Evaluate Appearance and its Effects 52
   Activate the Active Learner.. 53

Chapter 4: Determine Learning Styles and Use This Knowledge **53**
   Activate the Reflective Learner 54
   Balance Active and Reflective Learning 55
   Activate the Sensing Learner 55
   Activate the Intuitive Learner... 56
   Activate the Visual Learner... 57
   Activate the Verbal Learner... 57
   Activate the Sequential Learner 58
   Activate the Global Learner... 59
   Activate the Aural Learner.. 59
   Activate the Physical Learner.. 60
   Choose the Right Textbook and Materials 60
   Exercise: Identify Learning Styles 61
   Exercise: Evaluate Learning Methods.................................... 63

PART II: Getting Down to Business: What to Do Every Day **65**

Chapter 5: Read for Comprehension – General Reading Tips **67**
   Read Often 67
   Set a Pace 68
   Prepare Before Reading 69
   Look for an Organizational Pattern 70
   Focus on the Ideas... 70
   Take Steps to Reduce Zoning 71
   Master the Art of Skimming.. 72
   Recognize Signal Words 73
   Step Back in Time.. 74
   Apply the Material 74
   General Reading Skills Cheat Sheet....................................... 76
   Understand the Basic SQ3R System...................................... 77

Chapter 6: Read with a System – SQ3R and Beyond...................... **77**
   Exercise: Try It 79
   Build Upon the System 81
   Evaluate the Results... 84
   Forget What You Have Been Taught (In High School) 85

Chapter 7: Read with a Plan: Note-Taking Strategies **85**
   Beware of Used Books 86
   Love the Book.. 87
   Read First, Notate Later 88

Be Specific and Selective.. 89
Be Neat... 91
Copy onto Paper 91
Make Choices 93
Exercise: Create a System 94
Figure Out Why It Has Been Assigned....................................... 95

Chapter 8: Understanding Supplementary Materials..**95**
Do Not Dismiss Reading Strategies.. 96
Read the Chapter before the Lecture 97

Chapter 9: Get More out of Lectures..**97**
Ask One Question during Each Class Period............................... 98
Take Good Notes during Lectures... 99
Combine Textbook and Lecture Notes 100
Beat the Lecture Blues 101
Exercise: Examine What Makes Listening
During Lectures Difficult and Make a Plan to Counter Act It 102

Chapter 10: Recognize the Importance of Critical Thinking................................**105**
Understand the Importance of Lateral Thinking 106
Understand the Importance of Vertical Thinking 107
Balance Lateral and Vertical Thinking 108
Be Aware of Assumptions... 109
Practice Critical Thinking Skills 110

PART III : Putting It All Together: Proven Techniques for Exams **111**

Chapter 11: Prepare to Study...**113**
Allot Enough Time and Start Early 113
Organize the Material and Plan a Schedule 115
Predict Questions... 118
Utilize Provided Resources 121
Summarize and Condense... 125

Chapter 12: Active Studying Strategies **125**
Use Flashcards.. 130
Use Visual Depictions of Information 132
Create a Study Group... 133
Master the Review.. 134
Overcome Test Anxiety 137

Chapter 13: Plan a Test-Taking Strategy...**137**
Resist the Urge... 138
Read Directions 139
Prioritize and Budget Time 140
Use Every Second 141
Make the Right Choice... 143

Chapter 14: Take the Objective Exam...**143**
Find the Truth.. 146

Play Matchmaker 147

Chapter 15: Take the Essay Exam **149**

Chapter 16: Take the Open Book Exam **151**
Look at Mistakes 155

Chapter 17: Review Returned Tests **155**
Read and Understand Comments 156
Create a Study Log 158

PART IV: Completing Assignments **159**

Chapter 18: Understand Directive Words and Phrases **161**
Decipher Level One Directive Words 162
Decipher Level Two Directive Words 171
Decipher Level Three Directive Words 178
Handle Hybrid Directives 185
Research the Research Paper 187

Chapter 19: Special Considerations for Each Type of Assignment **187**
Start Early 191

Chapter 20: Allow Enough Time **191**
Choose a Prompt 193
Choose a Topic 194
Avoid Cramming In Regards To Research Assignments 195

Chapter 21: Research Early and Eagerly **195**
Find Credible and Current Sources 196
Know When to Stop 197
Specify the Search Terms 198
Think about Topics in Relation to Assignments 199

Chapter 22: Writing is Only a Small Portion of the Success **199**
A Thesis Is A Basis 200
Writing Process 202
Other Considerations for Projects, Papers, and Presentations 205

PART V : Handling Special Circumstances **207**

Chapter 23: Understand Online and Blended Classes **209**
Choose the Team 213

Chapter 24: Master Group Projects **213**
Take the First Step 214
Be the Leader 215
Delegate Tasks 216
Stay on Task during Group Meetings 216
Set Deadlines 218
Resolve Conflict 218
Pick up the Slack 220
Avoid Procrastinating 221

Chapter 25: Balance Extracurricular and Curricular Activities **221**

Make a List of Priorities 222
Get a Tutor 222
Utilize University Enforced Study Sessions.. 222
Look on On-Campus Jobs 223
Chapter 26: Balance Work and School...223
Stay Organized to Study Anywhere 224
Cut Back as Needed 224
Adjust Schedule 225
Chapter 27: Survive Finals Week 225
Attend Study Sessions 226
Stay Healthy 227
Avoid Stress.. 229
Stay Organized 230
Remember Studying and Test-Taking Strategies 230
Understand the Benefit 231
Chapter 28: Study Abroad 231
Choose a Program... 232
Make it Count 234
PART VI: Avoiding Studying Downfalls: How to Keep up with It All 235
Chapter 29: Utilize Offered Resources 237
Get Involved with Academic Departments 237
Frequent Tutoring and Writing Centers... 238
Look for Old Test Resources 239
Find out about Study Aids on the Internet 240
Visit Counseling Centers... 240
Read Professor Evaluations 241
Learn How to Access Databases for Research 241
Search for Specialty Libraries and Collections.. 241
Use Disability Services 241
Take a Writing Class 243
Chapter 30: Use First Year to Prepare for Rest...243
Take a Speech Class.. 244
Take a Tour of Campus with an Upperclassman 244
Examine Values 245
Chapter 31: Keep it Real..245
Define Personal Success... 246
Make Goals... 247
Stay Connected to Reality 248
Examine Majors and Minors Frequently 248
Know When to Transfer... 249
Keep a List 251
Chapter 32: Boost Your Concentration 251
Diagnose Which Classes Cause the Most Concentration Problems 252
Remove External Distractions 252

Avoid Multi-Tasking 253
Set Mini-Goals When Concentration is at Its Worst 253
When All Else Fails... 254
Make a Conscious Effort.. 255

Chapter 33: Improve Memory **255**
Exercise the Brain.. 256
Repeat and Recite 256
Create Acronyms 256
Visualize the Information.. 257
Write Sentences.. 257
Rhyme to Remember 258
Overload the Senses 258
Subscribe to a Word-of-the-Day Email...................................... 259

Chapter 34: Improve Vocabulary **259**
Learn Roots, Prefixes, and Suffixes.. 260
Keep a List of New Words.. 260
Read.. 260
Play... 261
Examine Lack of Motivation 263

Chapter 35: Stay Motivated **263**
Avoid Relying on Other People... 264
Stay Positive and Keep Things in Perspective............................ 264
Make Lists.. 265
Start Small 265
At this point, one of three things can happen: 266
Enroll in Summer School 267

Chapter 36: Maximize Summer and Semester Breaks...............**267**
Do an Internship.. 268
Volunteer 269
Anticipate the Learning Style 271

Chapter 37: Ease the Transition **271**
Ease the Fears... 272
Transitioning the Non-traditional Student 272
Set up a Meeting.. 275

Chapter 38: Approach the Professor **275**
Prepare for the Meeting... 276
Be Polite... 276
Keep Expectations in Check.. 276
Stay Open-Minded 277

Conclusion **279**

Bibliography **281**

About the Author..**283**

Index..**285**

PREFACE

Most college graduates fall into one of three categories. The first group of students spent almost all of their college career studying and had little time for fun or extracurricular activities. Those students typically graduate with honors and have tremendous academic success but didn't have much fun or make memories in college. The second group spent the majority of college partying, slacking off, and barely getting decent grades. The third group was able to do well in class and still have fun at the same time. They may or may not have graduated with honors, but they were successful in other facets of education, including extracurricular activities.

Students who are able to find the balance between academic life and social activities make the most of college and will look back with fond memories of learning and having fun. Social activities – whether it's hanging out with friends, involvement in extracurricular activities, or both – help students develop social skills and friendships that can rarely be found elsewhere. This is the time in their lives when they decide what is important, and if they spend all of their time studying and preparing for class, they won't acquire these essential life skills. On the other hand, college education determines their future and should be the basis of every decision.

A book about successful study habits in college isn't complete without discussing ways to become more organized and efficient—and this book does exactly that for you. This essential guide explains all the skills that students need to make the most of college, such as time management, organization, specific studying strategies, and taking advantage of college opportunities and learning experiences.

INTRODUCTION

I t's a typical scene that's depicted in dozens of movies. Incoming freshman complete all the necessary preparations before stepping foot on campus and feel that they're prepared for the next step in education. Because they're fresh out of high school, they'll most likely live in a residence hall and met new roommates. If they are non-traditional students, then they make other arrangements to receive their education. However, their preparations aren't complete.

Most freshmen anticipate and prepare for many changes and challenges in this new chapter of their lives, but they often overlook the difficulties of college. College isn't only about growing, changing, and having fun, but also learning, studying, and succeeding in the classroom. High school education is so much different from college; make sure you have that mentality on the first day of class, or you'll fall behind quickly.

According to a 2013 Politic365.com report, about 46 percent of students who attend college in the U.S. fail to graduate within six years. This statistic was 37 percent just a couple of years ago.

Students fail because college is difficult and different from their previous educational experiences. Statistics show that even the most successful high school students can have a difficult time when it comes to succeeding in college. Yes—the most intelligent student *can* fail in college.

The reason for this is two-fold. For many people, studying is not a natural hobby. It's a learned and practiced skill that works wonders for a student's future. Furthermore, the study skills and techniques necessary to succeed in high school are sometimes entirely different from college. This isn't to say that college students need to forget previous methods of studying; they just need to build upon and expand how they already study to adapt to the new environment. The second why students fail is because they have a skewed idea of college and don't expect anything that happens to them the first day, week, and semester. Because of this surprise, they are overwhelmed by what is expected and go from one extreme or the other. Some spend all of their time studying, which can burn them out quickly, whereas others skim through college without getting the most out of their experience.

Obstacles That College Students Battle

Let's take a closer look at why students fail in college:

Class Structure. In high school, most classes meet every day, so students have frequent contact with their teachers and time for a variety of activities including study sessions, work days, and other activities. In college, classes often meet only two or three times per week. Class is often dedicated to lectures, discussions, and other learning activities. Work and study sessions, including a fairly heavy load of reading, takes place outside of class in preparation for in-class activities. A class grade usually relies on a few activities, such as projects and tests, so all the "in-between" things (i.e. reading assignments, discussion questions, and quizzes) go un-graded. This is a difficult transition for students who expect to receive feedback on every assignment, and it also makes it easy for students to lose motivation or skip an assignment because "no one will know".

Schedules. In high school, students' schedules were jam-packed all day long with classes and possibly a study hall. Then students had their evenings to get other homework done and participate in other activities. In college, it's most likely that students will have classes scheduled throughout the day, with breaks in-between and different class times from one day to the next. It's often a difficult transition for freshmen to go from a dictated schedule to ultimate freedom.

Expectations. A professor or instructor's expectations are much higher than a high school teacher's. College students are expected to do a large percentage of independent work, and test material isn't always covered in class. Additionally, professors often try to elicit a higher level of critical thinking and problem solving from students, which takes more time and mental effort than high school-level work.

Distractions. There are so many distractions for new students, and they're probably the number one reason why students struggle with studying and doing well in college. There are new friends, new experiences, and new places to explore. This, paired with newfound freedom, makes it difficult for students to create good study habits.. Non-traditional students often face different challenges that demand more of their time, such as jobs and family responsibilities. Many college students don't take advantage of time between classes either. They often waste this time because "it's only an hour." Every small time increment adds up over the course of a week and could benefit your success in class.

Characteristics of Successful College Students

College graduates, on average, earn more over the course of their careers than non-graduates, so it's imperative that freshmen learn how to be successful students. With all these changes at hand, studying skills in college doesn't consist of taking notes or memorizing facts. Successful studying time for a college student encompasses a lifestyle that is designed for an individual, and by an individual, to help him or her have a well-rounded college education.

Even though each student has a unique learning style, the most successful college students have some of the following attributes:

Proactive Learning. Simply reading over information that will be on an exam or quiz is not enough to receive a high grade in a college-level course. Proactive learners take the initiative to read, write, think, and talk about the subject so they know and understand the subject matter, instead of only memorizing facts.

Self-Awareness. Successful college students have a high level of self-awareness when it comes to studying. This includes which subjects they are good at, what times of day they study the best, and what techniques and skills are the best tools to help them succeed. Successful college students also have a myriad of learning strategies available so they can pick the one that best fits a specific assignment.

Motivation. Motivation keeps a student going when college life becomes stressful. This perseverance includes attending class (even if it's at 8 a.m.), keeping up with assigned reading material, and putting in hard work. Students who take the initiative often have the drive and desire it takes to be successful in college.

Many college students don't naturally have these characteristics; these are learned skills. However, this book covers successful, necessary tips and tricks that teach active learning strategies, promote self-awareness, and foster motivation.

How to Use This Book

The goal of this book is to teach college students how to manage their time and master skills to help them study so they have the opportunity to *enjoy* college, not just endure it. This book is also a tool to help college students adapt to a new learning environment that is more demanding than anything they've experienced. The book also shows college students that being successful in college is much more than just getting an A. If students study quickly and efficiently, then they'll have time for extra opportunities in college.

Each student has different needs and reasons for reading this book. It's designed for easy access to specific areas of need. A good way to start is by reading the entire book. This will start you on the journey of a successful and enjoyable college experience. After an initial read-through, the book can be used as a point-by-point resource to help college students stay on track and refresh their skills in a slacking area. For example, if someone wants to work on time management, he or she can reread and implement the strategies in that particular section to help improve.

Scattered throughout the book are case studies that discuss common, bad college studying habits, as well as testimonies from real-life students that will make studying easier. Don't be afraid to try these tricks. They've already worked for someone else, and they may just work for you if you give them a try.

◇◇◇◇

PART I

SETTING YOURSELF UP FOR SUCCESS: WHAT TO DO RIGHT NOW

t doesn't matter who you are—studying doesn't happen naturally to anyone. Creating good study habits is a learned process that takes time, organization, discipline, and commitment. If you want to be successful, it's important to make studying more accessible and remove all possible distractions. Procrastination and laziness leads to problems such as cramming for a test in middle of the night or skipping classes to finish work for another. Getting these issues under control is the first step toward educational success.

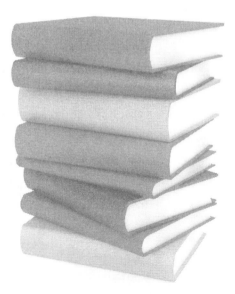

CHAPTER 1

MAKE A SCHEDULE

T ime management is a horrible word to most people. Designing and following a strict schedule is mind-boggling and confining for those who prefer to be scatter-brained. A successful student knows that a properly designed schedule can help even the busiest student stay on top of work and also have time to relax, unwind, and have fun without stressing about what still needs to be done tomorrow, the day after, or next week. This is possible because proper time management fits every class, task, and assignment, as well as downtime, into a well-balanced schedule.

It takes a little practice, but scheduling helps students fit in time with friends, regular workouts, and study breaks to watch a favorite television show without feeling guilty.

Here are some signs whether or not you need to use a scheduling system:

- You constantly cram for exams, write papers or complete projects at the last minute.

- You skip class to finish work from another class.

- You attend class but work on homework or study for another class.

- You often multi-task to get everything done. (It's never a good idea to read a textbook while running on the treadmill. You compromise both the workout and study session. They miss the stress-relieving, relaxing, and social benefits of working out, and they prevent themselves from actively reading the text.)

- You constantly make decisions between fun and work and feel guilty either way.

- Pulling all-nighters is the norm.

Determine Where Time Goes

Before writing a schedule, determine how you use time on a daily basis. Spend a few days keeping track of what you do all day, from the minute you wake up until you sleep. This will illustrate how you spend your time wisely and when you waste valuable time, too.

Many students are surprised about the amount of wasted time. It doesn't seem much in 10- to 20-minute increments, but time adds up quickly. One of the greatest benefits of writing down your original schedule shows the student how much time he or she has during the week. If this time is used efficiently, you can enjoy your downtime guilt-free. Another benefit includes seeing what "incidentals" are most important to the student, so he or she knows when and how to schedule their activities.

Below are some examples of information you might discover when you track your current schedule:

- You may determine you need an hour in the morning to wake up, have breakfast, and get ready for the day. This is something that should take priority on your schedule.

- Another student may find that studying between his or her afternoon classes doesn't work because of distractions and ends up daydreaming. This indicates that the time slot should be used for something else. It may be a good time for a break so she can do something she enjoys.

- Yet another student may realize that studying in the student union is a waste of time because, even though he is there for three hours every afternoon, he spends 75 minutes talking to friends.

- Another student may realize that, even though she spends an hour and a half at the cafeteria with her roommate and other friends, she feels revitalized enough to head back to the library for another few hours to study. She used to feel guilty about taking that break, but she now realizes it's vital for her.

Determine the Best Study Time

Most people concentrate better at different times of the day. Students should determine the best times to study, as well as when the worst times, so they can incorporate successful study blocks into their schedule.

Find out when you study the best by making note of the most and least efficient study sessions. This may change from day to day, depending on each day's schedule. Some students may have two relatively easy morning classes and are able to study mid-morning until their lunch break three days a week, but on the other two days, they may have two difficult, draining classes in the morning, so mid-morning study sessions aren't productive.

While this may change from semester to semester depending on your class load and schedule, it's important to note that most successful students are able to work between breakfast and dinner. Students usually socialize after dinner, and even if you have a quiet night, taking a break after dinner allows your body and mind to wind down from the day. Granted, this is not true for everyone, but those who can find time to study before dinner and relax in the evening are rejuvenated and ready when they wake up the next morning.

Other considerations to keep in mind when determining the best time to study:

- A favorite study spot across campus may mean that studying late at night isn't the best choice for someone who does not want to walk home alone.

- Some study spots are in buildings that close during certain hours, so they cannot be relied on throughout the day.

- Job schedules usually aren't consistent, so students will need to shuffle study times around depending on their schedules.

- Long classes, such as two- or three-hour night classes, can be draining; many successful students don't study heavily after this time.

- When your friends and roommates have free time is also important to consider. For example, if your friends keep Saturday afternoons open for hanging out, then you'll more than likely cancel a study session at the last minute to do something fun. Successful students take these things into consideration when making their schedules so they don't end up with a time crunch at the last minute and can still enjoy social activities with their friends.

Set Up a Regular Schedule.

Instead of setting up a schedule that has time slots indicated on the hour, make up a schedule template that follows the university's class schedule. If classes go from 8 to 9, 9:10 to 10:10, 10:20 to 11:20, 11:30 to 12:30, and so on, this is how your schedule should look on paper. At many colleges and universities, the Monday-Wednesday-Friday schedule is different than the Tuesday-Thursday schedule, so their weekly schedule should reflect the differences.

When setting up a schedule, it's important to add items whose times are set, such as classes, meetings, jobs, and anything else important (i.e. weekly dinner at a relative's house or a yoga class twice a week). It's also important to schedule times for fun and relaxation. Some students like to leave Sunday afternoon

open, for example. Others like to have one to two hours free every night. Your downtime should be scheduled during the times when studying is least effective.

Next, schedule study blocks. On average, successful students spend two hours a week studying for every hour per week spent in class. However, classes that are particularly demanding may require more time, and students who tend to read slowly should add more time as well.

Below are matters to consider when planning your successful schedule:

- Successful students start with classes and schedule everything else around those times.

- Successful students use their schedules to make the most of their time between classes. There usually isn't enough time to go home and come back to campus in time for the next class, so it's important to figure out how to use this time efficiently.

- Successful students recognize the importance of relaxation and taking the time to stay healthy, including exercising and eating right.

- Successful students often want to get more out of college than just a degree, so they join a club or organization and attend meetings and other functions, so these items also appear in the schedule.

- Successful students know when professors have office hours so they can stop by when they need to ask a question. While these aren't listed as time commitments on the schedule, they should be noted in case of haphazard events.

- Successful students also know when labs are available for student use. Again, these aren't listed on the schedule as commitments, but when they need to use them for class, the student doesn't need to waste time to see if they are open.

Commit to Going to Each and Every Class Meeting

Successful students go to class. Many professors say that unattended classes harm students' grades. Even if the class doesn't have penalties for missing class, students suffer solely by not attending and keeping up with class material. Many class periods offer invaluable discussions or information that cannot be replicated by copying someone's notes or reading the textbook.

Additionally, students who attend class and stick to their schedules are more likely to utilize their other time during the day wisely as well. Skipping a morning class to sleep in sets the student up to have a rushed, stressed, and "off" day because they haven't done their normal routine.

Professors like to see their students attend class. Here are some other benefits of attending class everyday:

- Successful students know they get a more thorough and internalized understanding of the subject when they are exposed to it on a regular basis.

- Successful students can get more out of class when they participate in the discussions and class activities led by the professor.

- Successful students can take advantage of the time immediately following class to ask the professor questions.

- Successful students get to know their professors more by attending class. Knowing their professors can help them, anticipate how they will grade, and what types of questions may be asked on an exam.

- The professors get to know the students who regularly attend class and will often be more understanding if and when the student is struggling with concepts in the class or if the student has an emergency and needs to miss class or make up an exam or assignment.

- Successful students avoid grade penalties from unexcused absences by attending all of their classes.

Plan Study Blocks

Putting time in your schedule for studying is important, but long blocks of time set aside for studying can seem daunting. Here are some tips to plan a balanced and successful schedule:

- **Take breaks:** Successful students often study for 50 minutes and then take a 10-minute break. Go for a walk, have a snack, chat with friends, check your social media accounts, or stretch and take a bathroom break.

- **Switch it up:** After the break, successful students change subjects or tasks. Reading the same textbook for hours and hours isn't effective.

- **Plan ahead:** Successful students bring all supplies and materials needed for the assignment or project. There is nothing worse than getting all set up to study then realizing that last week's notes are still at home.

- **Prioritize:** Successful students put their most difficult assignments at the top of the list for each study block so they can tackle these when their brains are still fresh.

Compensate for Special Circumstances

No time-management schedule will work without room for unplanned circumstances. There will be weeks when students have several exams and papers due. These weeks will obviously require more studying than other weeks. This is when students need to give up some of their downtime breaks. This may mean skipping dinner with friends and packing food to eat on a study break, recording their favorite show, or missing a workout. They may even need to study outside of their ideal study times. Occasionally, this higher degree of intensity is necessary, but successful students get through the extra workload without complete disruption to their lives.

There are also times when nothing goes your way. Students get sick or have emergencies that cause them to miss study breaks for a day or two. Sometimes, friends, phone calls, and other distractions take over. It happens to all students at one point or another. Try to minimize these occurrences, and rearrange other free time to make up for the skipped blocks.

Here are some other special circumstances that may cause a glitch in your schedule:

- A friend has an emergency and needs help.

- A boss has requested that all employees work more hours during an anticipated busy week.

- A professor announces a change in the syllabus, which adds an assignment or more material to read and study.

- A member of a group project is not pulling his or her weight, making the other members pick up the slack.

- A student feels the effects of stress and decides to take a "mental health day." Taking a break is okay once in awhile, as long as the student knows that there will be extra work to catch up on the next day. Sometimes, it's worth it.

- A special event, such as a concert, show, or club activity, takes precedence over studying one evening.

One way to manage weeks that have an extra workload due to multiple assignments, projects, or exams is to plan ahead. At the beginning of each semester, successful students take all of their syllabi and write the due dates for all assignments, exams, and projects on their schedules so they can see what is due at a glance.

Make Time for Fun

It's so easy for college students to get burned out quickly. This is why all college students need to make time for fun.

Using a schedule helps students visualize how they spend their time and allow them to make time for an intramural league or a club they previously thought they didn't have time for. There's more to college than just classes. Making memories and socializing are as important in helping students learn and grow during this time – as long as they keep it in balance.

While grades are important, so are other social activities that can be as much of a learning experience as an 8 a.m. lecture or afternoon lab.

Colleges and universities often offer a great variety of social activities and events for their students. Here is a list of free or cheap activities located on campus:

- Join an academic club or organization: Most university departments have discipline-related clubs and organizations. Students can also find honors societies and competition-based teams to join and make connections as well.

- Become a member of a social organization: These are clubs and organizations that aren't necessarily affiliated with a discipline on campus but appeal to leisure activities such as the outdoor club, poetry club, or film society.

- Take advantage of the university's resources: This includes art and history galleries, planetariums, theaters, and volunteer organizations.

- Make use of the student union: Student unions offer a variety of entertainment activities including outside performers (such as speakers, comedians, and musicians) and internal performers, such as students who like to perform.

- Try something new: Organizations on college campuses like to expose students to new things, such as an a cappella group, an independent film series, or speakers with varying viewpoints on political and social topics.

Students are informed about social happenings on campus by reading the university's publications, checking out information boards in the student union, events on Facebook, and asking around. On the same note, when students join organizations, they can help spread the word about these events to include others as well.

Make Use Of Your Breaks

The 10- to 15-minute breaks before class allow you to finish undone tasks that could potentially become much a larger problem if ignored.

Students with schedules know what needs to be done in the grand scheme of tasks, but days get hectic for everyone, so little assignments often go unnoticed. This is why successful students often jot down a list of matters that need to be done the next day. It may include returning a library book, meeting with a study group that doesn't usually meet, going to an appointment at the financial aid office, or picking up an application for an internship. It could also be a reminder to finish an assignment. This way, when students have a few spare minutes, they know what needs to be done.

There are many things students can do in this time, such as:

- Make a phone call: This is a great opportunity to call your parents and set up a visit home later in the month without worrying about being stuck on the phone. There is an easy out because class starts in a few minutes.

- Check your social media accounts: Sometimes, quickly checking your Twitter and Facebook turns into an hour online. Doing it before the next class allows for a quick check and few likes.

- See a professor: If the professor's office is nearby, students can stop by quickly to ask a question. If the answer will take longer than the time available, you can set up an appointment. At the minimum, you can set up an email conversation, and going to a professor's office is a great way for students to introduce themselves to their professors, especially in classes with hundreds of students.

- Get some fresh air: Just walking around outside before the next class starts can help a student clear his or her mind and revitalize a little bit before sitting for another hour or more.

- Have a snack: Students often have hectic schedules that make meals sporadic during the day. Healthy snacking between classes helps eliminate eating junk food as well as the inability to concentrate and fatigue that often accompany hunger.

- Run a quick errand: Students can use time between classes to run quick errands, such as stopping in the student union to pick up stamps or swinging by the library to return books.

- Organize: Students who arrive early to a class can use the time to go through their book bags and get rid of junk that accumulates.

Survive Those Crazy Weeks

Successful students who create a schedule and stick to it don't suffer as much during those "crazy weeks" – endless days filled with multiple exams, assignments, and projects– as those who don't manage their time. This is mainly because they've kept up with their classes all along, so there isn't as much cramming at the last minute. However, even the most organized students will feel the time crunch once in awhile. Here are tips to manage those strenuous weeks:

- **Stay healthy:** It's more important than ever for students to continue exercising and eating right so their bodies can function with the added stress of late nights and a huge workload.

- **Take breaks:** It may seem like there's no time for a break with so much work to do, but many successful students have found that when they aren't getting far in their work, it's time to take a break – even if it's for only 10 minutes.

- **Work ahead:** Having a schedule that clearly illustrates everything that is due on a certain day helps students prioritize and even get some work done early. There is no reason why a project or paper shouldn't be done the week before it's due to make time for studying the following week.

Exercise: Create a Schedule

Follow these simple steps to create a schedule that works for you:

1. *Determine how you spend your time and figure out what things are most important to you.*

List the five activities (other than studying and classes) that are most important to you.

A. _____

B. _____

C. _____

D. _____

E. _____

2. *Determine which times of the day are most efficient for you to study.*

Survey each of the following times to help determine which blocks are best for studying class material. Students who have schedules that vary from day to day may want to fill out this survey for each day. Another option is grouping days into similar schedules and completing the survey for each group.

Current Activities: If you use time before class to exercise every day, you may not want to change your schedule because your body is used to getting up and doing something active; it may be a difficult change if you decide to study during that time. Likewise, if your first class is at 8 a.m. and you currently sleep in until your class, it may not be a good time to study. However, if you get up early and lounge around waiting for class, this time may be used more efficiently.

Energy Levels: Some people have high energy levels in the morning, whereas others do at night. This is important to figure out because leisure activities should be completed during times of low energy, and studying should be completed during times of higher energy.

Concentration Levels: This may vary from day to day. For example, if a student has a mentally taxing class on Monday and Wednesday afternoons, he will likely have a low concentration level in the late afternoon on those days. Other days, late afternoon may be a great time for him to study.

Friends' Activities: While this should not always be a determining factor in your study schedule, it should have some impact. For example, if your friends spend every Thursday evening doing something together, such as dinner and a movie, it will be difficult to commit to a weekly study session at this time.

A.   Early morning (before your first class)

Current activities: _____

Energy level: _____

Concentration level: _____

Friends' activities: _____

B. Midmorning

Current activities: _____

Energy level: _____

Concentration level: _____

Friends' activities: _____

C. Midday (around lunch time)

Current activities: _____

Energy level: _____

Concentration level: _____

Friends' activities: _____

D. Afternoon

Current activities: _____

Energy level: _____

Concentration level: _____

Friends' activities: _____

E. Late afternoon (from about 3 p.m. until dinner)

Current activities: _____

Energy level: _____

Concentration level: _____

Friends' activities: _____

F. Evening (after dinner until about 9 p.m.)

Current activities: _____

Energy level: _____

Concentration level: _____

Friends' activities: _____

G. Night (after 9 p.m.)

Current activities: _____

Energy level: _____

Concentration level: _____

Friends' activities: _____

3. *Graph out a weekly schedule, make sure that time blocks follow your university's schedule, and add in all of your commitments, including leisure activities and study blocks. Some students like to use a color-coded schedule to help them see at a glance what type of activity they have scheduled.*

Here is a schedule for a 14-credit load: Notice the number of hours spent studying. In this instance, biology is a 5-hour-a-week class but doesn't require 15 hours a week of studying; the labs are largely in-class projects that don't require the 3:1 ratio of studying. Instead, this student decided to schedule a 1:1 studying ratio for the biology lab and lab review.

Monday	Tuesday	Wednesday	Thursday	Friday	Saturday	Sunday
Before 8 am	Before 8 am	Before 8 am	Before 8 am	Before 8 am	Before 8 am	Before 8 am
wake up/ get ready	7am yoga	7am yoga	7am yoga	wake up/ get ready	7am yoga	Sleep in Free Time
8am-9am	8am-9:30am	8am-9am	8am-9:30am	8am-9am	8am-9am	
Biology lecture	Biology lab	Biology lecture	Biology lab	Biology lab review		
9:10-10:10		9:10-10:10		9:10-10:10	9am – 10am	
Workout/ Shower	9:40-11:10	Workout/ Shower	9:40-11:10	Workout/ Shower	Study	
	Freshman Comp		Freshman Comp			
10:20-11:20		10:20-11:20		10:20-11:20	10am – 11am	
Study		Study		Study	Study	
11:30-12:30	11:30 – 1pm	11:30-12:30	11:30 – 1pm	11:30-12:30	12pm – 1pm	

Monday	Tuesday	Wednesday	Thursday	Friday	Saturday	Sunday
30 min lunch break Study	30 min lunch break Study	30 min lunch break Study	30 min lunch break Study	30 min lunch break Study	30 min lunch break Study	
12:40-1:40 Spanish I		12:40-1:40 Spanish I		12:40-1:40 Spanish I	1pm – 2pm Study	
	1:20 – 2:50 History 101		1:20 – 2:50 History 101			
1:50 – 2:50 Study		1:50 – 2:50 Study		1:50 – 2:50 Study	2pm – 3pm Study	
3:00-5:00 Study	3:00-5:00 Study	3:00-5:00 Spanish Study Group	3:00-5:00 Study	3:00-5:00 Study	3:00-5:00 Study	3:00-5:00 Study
5pm – 7 pm Study	5 pm – 6 pm	5 pm – 6 pm Study	5 pm – 6 pm Study	5 pm – 6 pm Study	5 pm – 6 pm Study	5 pm – 6 pm Study
	6 pm – 7 pm Dinner/Relax	6 pm – 7 pm Dinner/Relax	6 pm – 7 pm Dinner/Relax	6 pm – 7 pm Dinner/Relax	6 pm – 7 pm Dinner/Relax	6 pm – 7 pm Dinner/Relax
7 pm – 8 pm	7 pm – 8 pm	7 pm – 8 pm	7 pm – 8 pm	7 pm – 8 pm	7 pm – 8 pm	7 pm – 8 pm
After 8 pm	After 8 pm	After 8 pm	After 8 pm	After 8 pm	After 8 pm	After 8 pm

Key: **RED** = class, **BLUE** = study block, **GREEN** = leisure activities

Here is another example that uses color-coding for each class so students know what they should study during each study block. In this schedule, only classes and studying are written down with all open blocks signaling free time:

Monday	Tuesday	Wednesday	Thursday	Friday	Saturday	Sunday
Before 8 am	Before 8 am	Before 8 am	Before 8 am	Before 8 am	Before 8 am	Before 8 am
8am-9am	8am-9:30am	8am-9am	8am-9:30am	8am-9am	8am-9am	

Monday	Tuesday	Wednesday	Thursday	Friday	Saturday	Sunday
Biology lecture	Biology lab	Biology lecture	Biology lab	Biology lab review		
9:10-10:10		9:10-10:10		9:10-10:10	9am – 10am Study	
	9:40-11:10 Freshman Comp		9:40-11:10 Freshman Comp			
10:20-11:20 Study		10:20-11:20 Study		10:20-11:20 Study	10am – 11am Study	
11:30-12:30 30 min lunch break Study	11:30 – 1pm 30 min lunch break Study	11:30-12:30 30 min lunch break Study	11:30 – 1pm 30 min lunch break Study	11:30-12:30 30 min lunch break Study	12pm – 1pm 30 min lunch break Study	
12:40-1:40 Spanish I		12:40-1:40 Spanish I		12:40-1:40 Spanish I	1pm – 2pm Study	
1:50 – 2:50 Study	1:20 – 2:50 History 101	1:50 – 2:50 Study	1:20 – 2:50 History 101	1:50 – 2:50 Study	2pm – 3pm Study	
3:00-5:00 Study	3:00-5:00 Study	3:00-5:00 Spanish Study Group	3:00-5:00 Study	3:00-5:00 Study	3:00-5:00 Study	3:00-5:00 Study
5pm – 7 pm	5 pm – 6 pm Study	5 pm – 6 pm Study	5 pm – 6 pm Study	5 pm – 6 pm Study	5 pm – 6 pm Study	5 pm – 6 pm Study
	6 pm – 7 pm	6 pm – 7 pm	6 pm – 7 pm	6 pm – 7 pm	6 pm – 7 pm	6 pm – 7 pm
7 pm – 8 pm	7 pm – 8 pm	7 pm – 8 pm	7 pm – 8 pm	7 pm – 8 pm	7 pm – 8 pm	7 pm – 8 pm
After 8 pm	After 8 pm	After 8 pm	After 8 pm	After 8 pm	After 8 pm	After 8 pm

Key: RED = Biology, BLUE = Freshman Comp, GREEN = Spanish, Orange = History

CASE STUDY: THE ALL-NIGHTER

In the college world, some say that pulling an all-nighter is almost a rite of passage. When you first attended college, you were probably horrified when you saw the product of pulling an all-nighter on campus: barely functioning zombies who have dark circles under their eyes, chugging ungodly amounts of energy drinks, and are wearing yesterday's clothes. You may think, *that will never happen to me*, but by the time you're a senior, it most likely will.

Whether you're the most organized person or the worst procrastinator, you're bound to pull an all-nighter for an essay you forgot about or a test you've been putting off. You're a college student; it happens. You'd rather hang out with your friends or get distracted by the Internet. But pulling an all-nighter is a last-minute method that affects your health, grades and mentality.

Some students swear that all-nighters work for them, but this typically isn't true. Getting at least seven or eight hours of sleep every night keeps your mind fresh and alert. According to the U.S. National Library of Medicine and National Institute of Health, a lack of sleep affects your brain and slows down your ability to concentrate and communicate effectively. When you don't sleep, these symptoms can occur as well:

- Elevated levels of stress
- Weight gain
- Slow-working memory

- Emotionally irrational
- More prone to sickness

Pulling many all-nighters can affect your grades substantially. The following anonymous testimonials are from college students who pulled all-nighters themselves:

"I have crammed the night before a test and did well. I have crammed somewhere around five times."

"Yes, I have crammed several times. I've done excellent sometimes and also bombed a few tests."

"I've crammed, and I did not do well. I try to cram as little as possible."

There will always be split opinions and views on pulling all-nighters. Even though research shows the harmful side effects of it, college students continue to do them. As a freshman, you don't have to create this bad habit if you learn good study habits early on. Below are some solutions to getting your work done and not worrying about pulling an all-nighter:

- Dedicate at least an hour to homework every day

- Slowly work on essays, outlines and studying for upcoming tests days before they are due. Not only can you take your time, but you also can fit fun activities in between and not have to worry about the time crunch.

- Write out what needs to be done each day and set a small goal for yourself. This will keep you accountable.

Balancing college work and social time is extremely important. Don't ever work on an essay that's due the next day or study for a test at last minute. You just harm your body and risk failing. Plan ahead so you can avoid being another all-nighter statistic.

CHAPTER 2

◇◇◇◇◇◇◇◇

FIND A STUDY SPOT

The best advice successful students give when it comes to finding great study spots is: the more isolated, the better. Many college students have difficulty with procrastination. The best defense against it is to eliminate the distractions. Additionally, fewer distractions often allow for greater concentration.

Have Multiple Spots

There is nothing worse than studying for a huge, upcoming exam and finding out that your sacred study spot is taken. Circumstances like this can throw off your entire focus and ruin a study session, especially when you waste time searching for another good spot.

Here are some other reasons why successful students always have more than one study spot:

- Successful students choose several study spots around campus – preferably close to where they attend class – so they can easily pop in no matter where they are and don't have to trek across campus every time they want to study.

- Successful students know that they sometimes need a change of scenery. When this happens, they can pack up their things and head to the closest spot to re-focus on their studies.

- Successful students realize that good spots and areas are sometimes taken so it's best to find another place that's open and less distracting.

Know Which Spots to Avoid

Roommates and floor mates can be distracting. Dorms and apartments in general also provide a plethora of distractions, such as TV, organizing your room and anything else that could possibly be done, except for studying. It's not unusual for procrastinating students to suddenly have the urge to clean, wash dishes, or organize their desk. For these reasons, successful students know that serious studying must be done elsewhere, away from these distractions. They also know that dorms and apartments aren't the only areas that make poor study spots:

- Distracting areas are all over campus – large open areas full of tables and desks. They look like a great place to study, socialize and have a great time, right? These areas are great for catching up with friends and meeting with groups, but they are terrible for studying – focused studying, anyway. Successful college students avoid many distractions in these areas when they need to get work done.

- A great study spot in close proximity to your best friend's study spot is also a recipe for disaster. Studying close to a friend can result in endless chatter and little productivity.

- Some spots are too secluded. Students who tend to let their imaginations run wild shouldn't study in an area that is completely secluded. Before they know it, they've wandered off into their imagination and wasted precious studying time.

Know Where to Look

Finding secret study spots requires some searching and perseverance. Always be on the lookout for a good place to go. One place to start is in the library, but not in the main study areas. Instead, look for tables and desks tucked away in between shelves. Students may also find good study areas in small department lounges that many students aren't aware about— ask your professors if there is a student lounge or study room nearby.

Successful students choose study spots such as a classroom. Potential spots that aren't like a classroom environment may not be the best spots – even if they are secluded and quiet. Successful students often choose desks or tables with chairs over couches and other lounging furniture. Getting too relaxed while studying often diminishes their ability to concentrate and retain information. There are other clues that a study spot may not be as good as it first appears:

- Rooms that are too cold or too hot won't be comfortable for a long study session.
- Rooms that open easily to high traffic areas may not be good because they are prone to noise and the invitation of friends and acquaintances to stop in and chat.
- Rooms that are only open for short periods
- Rooms with plenty of windows can distract students, although this isn't true for everyone.

Keep a Secret

This is probably the hardest part but the most important – successful students keep quiet about these prime study spots. A few things can happen by spreading the word. First, other people will want to try out the spots and then they will become popular. Second, friends will start seeking you out in these spots, inviting distractions.

Exercise: Find and Evaluate Potential Secret Study Spots

Take a few hours to seek out a few good study spots. Start in the library away from community study areas and look in the stacks and other seemingly secluded areas. Then, move to the classroom buildings and look for lounges and other study rooms that might be unknown to most students.

List five potential secret study spots and evaluate them using the checklist that follows. Then, write down notes to help you remember important information about the spot such as when it's open (or closed) to the public or notes about the conditions such as "it's usually a chilly room, so bring a sweatshirt" or "noisy mornings when many students are in the building."

1. _____

- o   The spot is quiet.
- o   The spot is close to classes/dorm/apartment.
- o   The spot is in a building is regularly open to students.
- o   The spot is rarely occupied by other students.
- o   The spot is secluded.
- o   The spot is comfortable.
- o   The spot has plenty of space for spreading out work.
- o   The spot has outlets for a computer or other necessary electronic devices.

2. _____

- o   The spot is quiet.
- o   The spot is close to classes/dorm/apartment.
- o   The spot is in a building is regularly open to students.
- o   The spot is rarely occupied by other students.
- o   The spot is secluded.
- o   The spot is comfortable.
- o   The spot has plenty of space for spreading out work.

o   The spot has outlets for a computer or other necessary electronic devices.

3. _____

o   The spot is quiet.
o   The spot is close to classes/dorm/apartment.
o   The spot is in a building is regularly open to students.
o   The spot is rarely occupied by other students.
o   The spot is secluded.
o   The spot is comfortable.
o   The spot has plenty of space for spreading out work.
o   The spot has outlets for a computer or other necessary electronic devices.

4. _____

o   The spot is quiet.
o   The spot is close to classes/dorm/apartment.
o   The spot is in a building is regularly open to students.
o   The spot is rarely occupied by other students.
o   The spot is secluded.
o   The spot is comfortable.
o   The spot has plenty of space for spreading out work.
o   The spot has outlets for a computer or other necessary electronic devices.

5. _____

o   The spot is quiet.
o   The spot is close to classes/dorm/apartment.
o   The spot is in a building is regularly open to students.
o   The spot is rarely occupied by other students.
o   The spot is secluded.
o   The spot is comfortable.
o   The spot has plenty of space for spreading out work.

o   The spot has outlets for a computer or other necessary electronic devices.

Exercise: Plan Where You Will Study at Each Study Session

Go back to your schedule and plan where you will study during each session. It's best to note a back-up location just in case the preferred location doesn't work out. Here is an example from the previous schedule examples:

Monday	Tuesday	Wednesday	Thursday	Friday	Saturday	Sunday
8am-9am	8am-9:30am	8am-9am	8am-9:30am	8am-9am	8am-9am	
Biology lecture	Biology lab	Biology lecture	Biology lab	Biology lab review		
9:10-10:10		9:10-10:10		9:10-10:10	9am – 10am	
Workout/ Shower	9:40-11:10	Workout/ Shower	9:40-11:10	Workout/ Shower	Study Library, 3rd floor	
10:20-11:20	Freshman Comp	10:20-11:20	Freshman Comp	10:20-11:20	10am – 11am	
Study Student Lounge in For. Lang. Building		Study Student Lounge in For. Lang. Building		Study Student Lounge in For. Lang. Building	Study Library, 3rd floor	
11:30-12:30	11:30 – 1pm	11:30-12:30	11:30 – 1pm	11:30-12:30	12pm – 1pm	
30 min lunch break	30 min lunch break	30 min lunch break	30 min lunch break	30 min lunch break	30 min lunch break	
Study Student Lounge in For. Lang. Building	Study Library, 3rd floor	Study Student Lounge in For. Lang. Building	Study Library, 3rd floor	Study Student Lounge in For. Lang. Building	Study Library, 3rd floor	
12:40-1:40		12:40-1:40		12:40-1:40	1pm – 2pm	
Spanish I	1:20 – 2:50	Spanish I	1:20 – 2:50	Spanish I	Study Library, 3rd floor	
	History 101		History 101			

CHAPTER 3

GET ORGANIZED

Time management skills, perfect study spots, and the best study skills cannot aid college students if they are unorganized. Disorganization wastes time when you constantly search for supplies, paper, and other materials. You also lose focus when your mind is concentrated on finding misplace items. Successful students create a system that keeps everything together and easily accessible.

Organize the Backpack

Backpacks accumulate tons of junk, but successful students keep the miscellaneous pile to a minimum. Successful students also keep a few key items in their backpack, including extra paper, appropriate media supplies (such as flash drives), pens and pencils, spending money, and a few emergency snacks. This, in addition to the textbooks and notebooks for each class, should be enough to sustain any successful student for classes and study sessions throughout the day.

Successful students have their own quirks when it comes to studying. Some like to listen to classical music to drown out white noise, whereas others keep a stress ball handy. Some successful students have one musician they listen to only when studying which helps them drown out distractions and get down to business. Whatever the quirk, successful students keep necessary supplies in their backpacks at all times.

In addition to these items, successful students also know it's important to keep a stash of handy supplies in their bags "just in case." These include:

- A mini stapler
- A calculator
- Sticky notes – preferably different colors
- Notepads and notebooks
- Pens and highlighters in several different colors
- A water bottle
- Spare change
- Ear plugs – for those times when it is impossible to find a quiet place to study
- Headphones (for music or to block out noise)

Organize the Papers

Each student needs to find an individual, easy-access method for organizing class materials. Some students need large binders to hold all syllabi, notes, and other materials for each class, as well as a master schedule for the semester. These students often take notes on loose-leaf paper in class and then pop them into the binder in the proper section at the end of class. This also allows the students to put handouts and other materials from class right before or after the notes relating to them. Another benefit is that students can combine or align class and lecture notes with notes more easily than if they were taking notes in a spiral-bound notebook. This is a great method for some students when they want to keep everything together.

Not everyone likes this method because binders can be bulky, and students don't always prefer carrying every class note with them if they don't need it, or they prefer notebooks to loose leaf paper because it's less likely to get lost or disorganized. Here are some other options:

- Successful students who like using binders but don't like having all of their class materials in one large and heavy binder, tend to use one smaller binder for each class. This way, they can keep all class information organized and only need to carry binders for the classes they'll work on that day.

- Other successful students benefit from color-coding. This means that all binders, notebooks, and folders for every class are a different color. Some even go as far as using sticky notes and media components, such as flash drives, which are color-coded as well.

- Within binders and folders, some students like to organize their materials by date, whereas others prefer organizing it by topic.

Dress for Success

It's tempting for many students to dress in sweats and other comfortable clothes when they are getting ready for a long study session, but successful students have found that this isn't always best. When students wear sweats and other comfortable lounging clothes, they often feel less like studying and more like partaking in leisure activities. This doesn't mean that successful students wear business attire or other formal clothing to class or for studying, but they should get up and get ready for the day. Besides, most students agree that if they feel good about themselves, they often do better when it comes to school, work, and studying.

Appearance <u>does</u> matter:

- Students who dress for class make a better impression on their professors.

- Students who get dressed tend to be more energetic and willing to get to work done even during "down" time.

- Students who dress for class make a better impression on their classmates and are taken more seriously in study groups and other group activities.

- Human nature shows that people strive to meet expectations set upon them. Students who care about their appearance and strive to make a good impression on others soon find that other people have higher expectations of them. Likewise, lower expectations are set on those who don't show that they care about their appearance.

Exercise: Organize Study Supplies

Successful students aren't afraid to dump their backpack and clean out their mess. Don't wait—do this now. Dump everything out, get rid of trash, and start organizing. Make sure your backpack contains all necessary supplies. The following is a checklist of items that should always be in your backpack:

o   Extra paper
o   Flash drives
o   Pens (in various colors)
o   Pencils and a pencil sharpener

o High-lighters (in various colors)

o Spending money

o Student ID

o Snacks

o Mini stapler

o Tape

o Sticky notes (in several colors)

o Calculator

o Water bottle

The following items are useful, but not necessary for successful studying. Decide what is most important to you and find a spot for them in your bag:

o An iPod (or music from your phone or computer)

o Earplugs

o Stress ball

o Any other item that makes studying more successful for you

Exercise: Organize Class Materials

Additionally, this is a great time to evaluate your organization system for class materials. If it's non-existent or not working, make a new plan.

In the space below, write down how you currently organize your class materials and answer the following questions:

_____

_____

_____

_____

_____

Do you ever find yourself searching for class materials because you don't know where they are? If so, you need to reorganize your information.

Do you sometimes or often forget class materials that you need for a specific study session? If so, you need to plan your day the night before so you have everything you need with you.

Do you like to carry all of your class materials with you all the time? If so, a binder method may work well for you.

Do you like to organize your material by topic? If so, you may want to look into using loose-leaf paper instead of notebooks.

Do you sometimes grab the wrong folder or notebook for a certain class? If so, you may want to color-code your class materials for easy identification.

Write out three things you are going to do today to help improve your organization skills:

1._____

2._____

3._____

Exercise: Evaluate Appearance and its Effects

Try this for a week. Get up every morning, get dressed in something other than pajama bottoms or sweats, and see what difference it makes. Spend a few minutes every night before bed evaluating your energy level, concentration and overall mood.

CHAPTER 4

DETERMINE LEARNING STYLES AND USE THIS KNOWLEDGE

Successful students know their best learning styles and how to use these styles to their advantage. There are many different learning styles and various theories to go along with them.

Activate the Active Learner

According to Richard M. Felder and Barbara A. Soloman's article, "Learning Styles and Strategies," active learners need to use information at hand to be able to internalize, remember, and understand learning material. They learn most successfully through discussions and practical applications. Active learners struggle in classes that consist primarily of lectures because they don't have the opportunity to discuss or internalize information to understand it. According to Felder and Soloman,

active learners need to take the extra initiative to make up for this lack of active learning in order to be successful. Suggestions for this include:

- Organizing a study group
- Explaining concepts to others
- Simulating problem-solving exercises
- Asking the professor for ideas of activities that can help them actively process information
- Seeking out free websites, study aids (such as Smokin' Notes), and learning centers that can help them put information to practical use
- Attending tutoring sessions that allow groups to actively discuss topics with professors or teacher's assistants

Activate the Reflective Learner

Reflective learners think about information before talking about it or putting it to use, preferring solitary learning time. Reflective learners often struggle in fast-paced classes that don't allow time for slowly processing information, such as a lecture, discussion, or lab that takes an entire class period. As Felder and Soloman point out, reflective learners can do activities that give them extra time to think about information:

- Contemplate assigned readings before class so they have a basic idea about what will be discussed.
- Review the reading assignment several times before class.
- Think about the material before and after class, figure out practical applications, and individually simulate problems and solutions related to the topic.
- Spend time comparing notes taken in class with those from the text, drawing connections and creating summaries.
- Take time after class to sit quietly and digest the information. Some students find this most helpful if they look over notes and add thoughts and other ideas while they reflect.

Balance Active and Reflective Learning

Felder and Soloman state that most students are both active and reflective learners in different scenarios. Students have a strong, moderate, or mild affinity toward one or the other; however, having a solid balance between both is best. Too much active learning can lead to problems in a project or study session, and too much reflective learning can cause students to spend too much time thinking and not enough "doing."

There are ways to achieve this balance:

- Active learners can study with reflective learners, as long as they are both open to the other's perspective.
- Active learners can purposefully make themselves slow down and think about the topic before jumping right in and doing whatever needs to be done.
- Reflective learners can set aside a time limit for thinking about the topic before they begin their work.

Activate the Sensing Learner

Felder and Soloman state that sensing learners prefer learning facts and solving problems with tried-and-true methods. Sensing learners also memorize and complete lab-type work that has a specific procedure. Overall, sensing learners are practical and need to see how a specific class applies to the real world and struggle in classes if they don't see a clear connection to practical uses.

To expand their learning style, sensing learners should:

- Ask the professor for clarifications.
- Attend a class discussion group where the members brainstorm real-world connections to help them internalize information.
- Spend time making real-world connections.
- Seek out additional sources that may have more information on how topics apply to the real world.

- Use examples from the text as a jumping board to create individual examples.

Activate the Intuitive Learner

According to Felder and Soloman, intuitive learners absorb information the best through discovery and dislike repetition. Intuitive learners quickly understand new concepts and are often innovative in their studies. Intuitive learners dislike the courses that require memorization and participation in repetitive work.

Intuitive learners are fairly lucky in college because the majority of classes require this type of thinking and application of concepts any way. Professors often require innovative application of class material instead of memorization and repetition of facts. There are exceptions to this, however, when intuitive learners find themselves in classes that require a large amount of memorization and repetitive work. Intuitive learners are often bored and make careless mistakes on exams and assignments because they don't like repetitive questions. There are steps that prevent problems in repetition-oriented classes, such as:

- Make an effort to pay special attention to the details, especially when completing exams and assignments.

- Ask for recommendations of professors who you'll learn well from before signing up for classes. There will be some classes and professors who can't be avoided, however, due to the nature of the subject matter.

- Spend extra time thinking about different ways the information can be used so you have an idea of what type of purpose it serves while you do repetitive work for class.

Activate the Visual Learner

Felder and Soloman define visual learners as those who need to observe graphics to understand the material – such as pictures, timelines, demonstrations, films, and flow charts. Visual learners need to see how a word looks when they try to spell it.

Visual learners struggle in predominantly verbal classes. They can take extra steps to alleviate some of the stress and problems, however, by:

- Seeking out supporting materials for the text, such as websites that contain more beneficial information. Some textbooks also have companion books available that contain maps, graphs, pictures, and other graphics to go along with the information.
- Take notes in the form of concept maps, graphs, charts, and timelines instead of outlines or lists.
- Use colored pens and highlighters to color-code notes and make them more visually appealing.
- Create charts and other graphics from the reading in anticipation of what the lecture will be about to visualize the information.
- Keep the textbook handy during lecture so you can look at graphics while the professor discusses the topic.

Activate the Verbal Learner

Verbal learners easily express themselves in a written or spoken context because they understand information based on what they get out of spoken and written words. Verbal learners are lucky when it comes to college classes, but they can still learn more skills to improve their learning style. Verbal learners should take notes and write down key concepts and ideas in their own words. They can also benefit from the following:

- Participating in study groups that discuss and explain the topics
- Reading, writing, and playing word games
- Using mnemonics to remember facts
- Creating rhymes and rhythms to remember facts and concepts
- Writing and rewriting notes
- Reciting information

While individual students prefer either visual or verbal (visual learning usually takes precedence over verbal learning, according to Felder and Soloman), most students learn best with a mixture of both. This is bad news for college students because classes rely on little visual information during discussions and lectures.

Activate the Sequential Learner

Felder and Soloman state that sequential learners figure out concepts in a logical, step-by-step fashion. Sequential learners find solutions by following a set of formulas – even if they do not fully understand the information. The sequential learner is also called 'the logical learner'. These students lean toward subjects like math. They also rely on lists, which can be useful when studying for an exam. Sequential learners often have a difficult time in classes where the professor tends to jump around or doesn't fully explain all the steps. Sequential learners need to fill in the missing information by asking their professor or seek out the information outside of class. Other steps they can take to improve their learning include:

- Spending time after each class reorganizing notes into logical and sequential lists
- Joining a study group to discuss the missing areas of information and clarify facts

- Referring to the textbook often to help them visualize the steps in the process
- Finding additional resources to help them fill in the blanks in their notes (i.e. asking the professor or looking for reference material in the library or online)

Activate the Global Learner

Global learners learn in a random manner because they tend to work with large chunks of information and eventually just "get it." Global learners often have a difficult time explaining how something works once they figure it out or how they got to the solution.

Global learners need to see the big picture before they can internalize information. They can feed their learning style by seeing the big picture before delving too deeply into the details. This includes the following steps:

- Skimming a chapter before fully reading it so they can anticipate what is coming up next
- Paying attention to the syllabus so they can see how each class's topics relate
- Writing down the thought processes that led up to figuring out how something works so they can replicate it in the future
- Pairing up with sequential learners who may be able to help them see how all the details contribute to the solution instead of just looking at the big picture

Activate the Aural Learner

Aural learners are those who learn best with sound. This can mean rhyming, music, or listening to the content. Aural learners sometimes benefit by reading their notes into a tape recording and then listening to them again and again. Aural learners also benefit from using mnemonics and jingles– such as changing the words to a popular song to fit the information being studied. They can use their preferred learning style to their advantage by using the following techniques:

- Choosing classes that are lecture-based (whenever possible)
- Studying in areas that allow them to recite notes and listen to recordings of notes
- Participating in discussion groups
- Looking for auditory supplements to the text, such as sound recordings

Activate the Physical Learner

The physical learner needs to work with his or her hands to be able to internalize the information. Physical learners need demonstrations and the ability to participate in the process. Even when physical objects are not available for manipulations, physical learners should try the following suggestions:

- Rely on writing and drawing –use large paper to make big drawings and words.
- Act out the process or concepts, such as role-playing events in history.
- Ask the professor for help in finding manipulators related to the topic.
- Create models and dioramas that depict the topic.

Choose the Right Textbook and Materials

Professors choose the textbook for the class, but successful students take advantages of choices within the textbook. Textbook publishers often offer online supporting material – often in the form of slideshows, graphs, diagrams, maps, and other visuals. These items are included in new books or can be purchased separately. Furthermore, an increasing number of publishers now offer an Internet code with the purchase of new books to allow students to access supporting materials online. Students who have questions about this should speak to a university bookstore representative or to professors to get more information about the materials.

Students who embrace their learning styles and try out the previous recommendations will soon use their study time more efficiently. They will enjoy studying more if they choose activities that help them learn better. Before long, efficient studying will make them enjoy the subject matter, even if it's a previously disliked class.

Exercise: Identify Learning Styles

Use this quick guide to determine which learning style(s) you use. Read through the characteristics in each section and highlight the section(s) that best describe your studying and learning tendencies. Once you have completed this, use the key to identify your learning styles.

Learning Style A	Learning Style B
• Prefer classes that involve memorization and other information. • Need to know how the information/topics/concepts apply to the practical world to fully understand its importance.	• Learn better with visual depictions of the information such as a timeline, chart, graph, or demonstration. • Struggle in classes where the information is provided through lecture with minimal use of visual aides.
Learning Style C	**Learning Style D**
• Can see the whole picture but often the details are fuzzy. • Know the answer or solution to a problem but often cannot explain the steps to reach that solution. • Need to be able to see the big picture before thinking about how the details fit together.	• Prefer classes that require or allow hands-on applications of the material. • Like to see demonstrations but prefer to participate in the process. • Use physical objects or manipulators to help learn a concept. • Role-play or act out scenes to help internalize information.

Learning Style E	Learning Style F
• Can easily express ideas through writing and speaking. • Prefer lectures versus demonstrations and labs. • Enjoy working with study groups that focus on discussing the information.	• Like to use music, rhyming, or other rhythmic methods to help remember information. • Enjoy lecture-based classes. • Benefit from taping notes and listening to them repeatedly.
Learning Style G	Learning Style H
• Need to use the information to understand it. • Like to discuss information with teachers and classmates. • labs, practical application, and discussions versus lectures.	• Prefer to use formulas to find answers and understand concepts. • Use lists and other step-by-step formulas for studying and understanding the material.
Learning Style I	Learning Style J
• Need time to think about information before discussing or applying it. • Prefer studying alone versus studying with a group. • Dislike participating in class discussions if there's no time to digest the information first.	• Dislike classes that require memorization and other information. • Become bored with classes that require the repetitive use of concepts and formulas. • Prefer to learn through discovery instead of receiving information upfront.

Key: A = Sensing, B = Visual, C = Global, D = Physical, E = Verbal, F = Aural, G = Active, H = Sequential, I = Reflective, J = Intuitive.

List up to four preferred learning styles below (if you have more than four highlighted in the chart, try to narrow it down to your top four).

1._____

2._____

3._____

4._____

Exercise: Evaluate Learning Methods

In the following table, list your current classes at the top of the blank columns. In the rows, list your preferred learning styles. Then, in each space, list two or three specific things you can do to utilize your learning style preference to succeed in your class.

	General Tips	Class #1	Class #2:	Class #3:	Class #4:
Learning Style #1					
Learning Style #2					
Learning Style #3					
Learning Style #4					

CASE STUDY #2: MYTH BUSTED: "EVERYONE LEARNS THE SAME WAY."

CLASSIFIED CASE STUDIES ™

directly from the experts

One of the most inhibiting factors for students' success is understanding class material and doing well on exams. Each professor teaches his or her class differently and doesn't cater to an individual student's needs. That's why figuring out your specific learning style is so vital; you'll be much more successful in the classroom if you study efficiently the first time.

Some students are **auditory**, **kinesthetic** or **visual** learners; sometimes, students are a mixture of both. Most professors lecture, which makes auditory learners succeed in the classroom. As for the other learners, they may struggle to keep up. Kinesthetic learners need to have hands-on experiences and write things down in order to succeed. Visual learners must read, look at diagrams and watch demonstrations.

The best way to figure out what type of learner you are is by testing different studying methods: paying attention to lectures without writing anything down, taking notes and rereading them, applying topics to real-life scenarios, outlining, taking practice test, making flashcards and attending lecture reviews. After you go through all of these and other strategies, determine which ones would the best for you.

Below are testimonies from college students who figured out their personal learning style:

Anna Den Adel, *"I've tried many different study methods, and practicing examples/old tests over and over again works best. Studying by breaking up the material by sections to study each day before the exam always gets me the best results."*

Zachary Humphrey, *"I tend to be visual and kinesthetic. I read the book and then write down notes, and then I read my notes. It didn't take me long to figure it out - I discovered it just by taking notes in class in middle and high school."*

Camille Harakal, *"I am a visual learner I have found. I like to write and rewrite everything I need to know, often grouping important subjects or aspects at a time."*

Nobody learns the same way; it's very normal to learn differently from your friends. The sooner you discover how you study the best, the sooner you will be successful in the classroom.

Some solutions to enhancing your newly discovered learning style include reading research articles related to the learning style and trying new strategies. Knowing how you study the best will make your life so much easier and eliminate future frustration and issues. If you're still not sure what type of learner you are, you can also ask a specialist for more help.

PART II

GETTING DOWN TO BUSINESS: WHAT TO DO EVERY DAY

S tudying is more than hitting the books the night before a quiz or exam or quickly throwing together a project. Successful students know that if they study a little each day, then they'll be under much less stress than putting assignments off until they're due the next day or in a few hours. Keeping up with the little readings and assignments makes studying for midterms and writing 6,000-word papers easier when they're due.

CHAPTER 5

READ FOR COMPREHENSION – GENERAL READING TIPS

College classes require a plethora of reading that can be overwhelming and seemingly impossible. Furthermore, many students feel like reading is a waste of time in general. Reading your class material is mainly required for tests and not always discussed in class. The following tips will help students improve their reading comprehension:

Read Often

Successful students read frequently. This builds up a wealth of knowledge to understand and apply concepts when reading for a class. Reading can be a leisure activity, whether it's fiction or non-fiction. You can read a book, newspaper, or even the Internet. As long as it's building up knowledge, anything you read

is beneficial. Students who constantly read usually display the following characteristics:

- They tend to know about current events.
- They can relate subject matter to other topics.
- They have a broader base to build their new knowledge.
- They read more efficiently than counterparts who don't leisurely read.
- They have a hobby they can do virtually anywhere –between classes and on the go.
- They build their vocabulary, which helps with reading comprehension.

Set a Pace

Successful students create a certain pace that helps them read every reading assignment as quickly as possible without compromising comprehension of the material. This pace differs for everyone. Students also need to re-evaluate their reading pace often so they don't go too fast or slow.

Successful students know that a reading pace needs to be flexible. Depending on the material, they may read the text faster or slower than the previous assignment. The time of day and level of distractions can affect reading speed as well. This is why it is important to continually evaluate the success of the reading and adjust whenever necessary. Your reading pace may be too fast if you're having these problems:

- Rereading the text over and over
- Not finding any main points in large portions of the text
- Promptly forgetting what you read
- Not fully understanding the discussed concept
- Not sure which information needs to be reviewed

The reading pace may be too slow if the student is having these problems:

- Consistently writing more notes than will fit into the margin
- Inability to keep the flow of the text going or difficulty connecting information from one section to another
- Becoming bored with the content

Prepare Before Reading

One of the best ways to get the most out of reading is establishing a basis of the assigned reading contains. This can be done in several ways. Successful students use the following techniques:

- Looking over the layout, including what types of external material is found in sidebars, charts, graphs, and margins.

- Evaluating the length of the chapters. Successful students are often proactive against getting bogged down and bored with a topic by following the rule of ten, meaning not reading more than ten pages of a chapter in one sitting. Breaking down chapters makes reading the material easier because a 10-page chapter sounds better than a 40- or 50-page chapter.

- Skimming through several pages to see what the reading contains.

- Reading the introduction, conclusion, and summaries.

- Looking for a pattern of typographical cues. Words and ideas that are bolded, italicized, underlined, or placed in a bulleted list are words and ideas the author emphasizes. These are important ideas that need special attention. Knowing how the author uses these cues will help the student anticipate what to look for. Successful students know they need to figure out why these items are highlighted and fit them into the bigger picture of the meaning in the text.

- Thinking about what they are going to read before they read it. Successful students look through the textbook and read headings and subheadings. While doing this, they think about what they already know about the subject. This helps them anticipate what they will be reading; it also helps them generate questions about what they would like to know.

This process doesn't have to be time consuming. It can be done in as little as five minutes, and once a student has a feel for a book, the basis doesn't need to be reestablished. However, some students do a "mini" preparation at the beginning of each chapter to give them an overview of a chapter.

Look for an Organizational Pattern

The reading assignment will have an organizational pattern. Students who familiarize themselves with the organizational pattern before reading will have a better sense of what to expect as they read. Possible types of organizational patterns include listing a sequence, following a process, progressing through a place, listing items by importance, comparing multiple items, or listing cause-and-effects.

Anticipating the organizational pattern helps students with the following tasks:

- Figuring out how they are going to organize their notes
- Anticipating when and where their questions will be answered in the text
- Systematically working their way through the text
- Picking out the most important topics
- Getting a sense for how the author approaches the information

Focus on the Ideas

Successful students admit that it's sometimes difficult to see the whole picture, but when they take the time to focus on the text's ideas in a paragraph, page, or chapter, it's easier to recall the facts and details later. By focusing on the specific details while reading, some students fail to see the whole picture and main ideas. Successful students use different techniques to help them keep their focus on the ideas instead of the small details. These techniques include the following:

- Allowing themselves to only write one phrase or idea per paragraph
- Reading several paragraphs before writing anything down
- Asking and answering questions about the text (more about this later)
- Reviewing and revising notes that contain keywords while thinking or reciting the facts
- Using concept maps or other visual guides to connect ideas
- Reading the conclusion to see how the author connects and applies the ideas in the reading

Take Steps to Reduce Zoning

Even the most successful students can zone out while reading. It's easy to do and becomes frustrating because they have to reread. Here are some tips that successful students incorporate when they read:

- Read with intonation (reading the text as if it was spoken aloud). This technique is useful because it requires the reader to actively understand what is written and how it should sound rather than mindlessly scanning the words. Reading with intonation also makes reading more memorable because it adds feeling and emotion to the text – and it can even help the reader get a sense of the personality of the writer based on how the words sound and come together.

- Take breaks. Successful students know the importance of giving themselves mental breaks. If your eyes and mind get blurry, then it's a good time to take a break and switch to a different subject or assignment.

- Make a list. Zoning out while reading means students are thinking about other things instead. When this happens, successful students take a minute to make a to-do list, whether it's what they need to pack for a weekend trip or get at the grocery store later that afternoon. Writing running thoughts will clear your mind.

Master the Art of Skimming

Although skimming is one of the steps that successful students use to help them become acquainted with the textbook and reading assignment, there are times when skimming should take precedence over reading word-for-word:

- Skimming is appropriate when the student searches for something specific.

- Skimming is a great way to review material, especially when a student answers questions about the reading assignment and needs to refresh his or her memory on what was in the section.

- Skimming can be beneficial if the student is fairly knowledgeable about the topic and wants to make sure there isn't any new information provided.

- Skimming helps students clarify misunderstandings in their notes or discrepancies between notes taken from the text and notes taken during a lecture. It helps the student quickly find the area where the specific topic is discussed.

Warning: Skimming is not a good idea for any students who are reading for comprehension.

Recognize Signal Words

Successful students look for signal words while reading to anticipate the main points. Walter Pauk illustrates these words in his book, *How to Study in College.* Here are some of the examples:

- Words that indicate examples are "specifically," "for example," "for instance," and "to illustrate." These words are clues that students should understand before deciphering the example.

- Words that indicate cause-and-effect are "consequently," "as a result," "accordingly," and "hence." These words are clues that the effect is about to be illustrated. It is important for students to understand the causation.

- Words that indicate enumeration – "first," "second," and "third" – tell the student they need to make sure they understand all the steps in the process being illustrated.

- Words that indicate contrast such as "on the other hand," "however," and "despite," tell the student to make sure they understand both sides of the issue.

- Words that indicate comparisons are "likewise," "similarly," and "identical." These words tell students that two things are similar.

Step Back in Time

Successful students who study a difficult subject, concept, or read a book that is difficult to understand, should look elsewhere for clarification. This concept works well for topics in science and history – check out children's or young adult's books on the topic to get a basic idea of the subject. Often, this gives students enough background information to understand the book.

Here are some great series of books that can be used for background information on topics:

- *Opposing Viewpoints* from Greenhaven Press Publishing: This series offers books on a variety of social topics, and each contains articles about various sides of issues. They promote critical thinking about the topic at hand.

- *The We Were There* series gives real-life accounts of people in history. Each book focuses on a different event, time period, or issue in history.

- *The Magic School Bus* is a series of fictional books that explores a science theme or topic in each book. Children board the magic school bus with their teacher and find themselves in predicaments that use science knowledge to solve problems and get back home.

Apply the Material

Successful students often do more than read and take notes. They take time – not necessarily immediately after finishing readings – to process information and find ways to apply it to their lives. For example, if they just finished reading a math textbook that explained the theory behind a certain math function, they may spend time figuring out how this specific math function actually applies to their lives and how they may use it, other than to just pass the upcoming assignments and exams. Successful students also apply the material to their lives by:

History

- Students put themselves in the middle of a historic event. This includes examining feelings and anticipating actions. It can also include practicing problem-solving skills to determine how and why people made the decisions they made.

- Thinking about what they would have liked or disliked about living in that time period.

English

- Thinking about a fictional piece, putting themselves in the middle of the story, and examining how they would react in such a situation. Other ways to apply fictional work to their lives is determining who they would be friends or enemies with, what advice they would give the characters, and what their reactions to situations would be versus the reactions of the characters in the book.

- Examining how they use grammar and other English topics on a regular basis and trying to implement one change at a time.

Foreign Language

- Trying to add one or two new phrases from what they read into their daily vocabulary for a few days until they know what it means and how to use it.

- Comparing their own lives with the culture(s) they read about. This includes comparing, contrasting, and examining how they would feel living in other cultures.

Science

- Thinking about how the concepts relate to their daily lives. Thinking about how the studies and research related to the concept improve their lives.

- Developing hypotheses on how the concepts could be used to solve problems they face on a regular basis.

General Reading Skills Cheat Sheet

Read Often	Expand knowledge, apply material, improve reading speed, a portable hobby, and increase vocabulary
Set a Pace	Adjust when rereading too often, when not finding main points, when forgetting what has been read, and when not understanding concept
Prepare First	Understand layout to help predict what will be next, think about length of sections, and observe typographical cues
Look for Patterns	Understand the texts organization to help organize notes, anticipate questions and answers, and find main points
Focus on Ideas	Avoid getting hung up on the details and try to look at the whole picture first
Skim	Help find specific information and prepare for a review
Signal Words	Recognize and understand the importance of words that signify important information
Simplify Information	Use children and young adult texts to clarify a concept before delving into the more complicated details present in college-level texts
Use Resources	Clarify misunderstandings and other confusions with the library's resource section
Apply the Material	Think about how and why this information is important in real life

CHAPTER 6

READ WITH A SYSTEM – SQ3R AND BEYOND

During World War II, Francis P. Robinson designed the SQ3R system to help military personnel read and study faster. A proven, successful system, SQ3R had some drawbacks that led students to modify the steps to fit their needs better.

Understand the Basic SQ3R System

The basic SQ3R system asks students to take five steps when reading and understanding a text: **Survey, Question, Read, Recite, and Review**.

- In the **Survey** step, students preview the text and get a feel for how the information is organized. They also read through the headings, subheadings, summaries, and conclusions. This step should be quick – students should be able to survey the text in a minute or two and get a sense of what ideas will be covered overall. It also helps the students mentally organize the material as they are reading it, because they know what has been covered and what will be covered.

- In the **Question** step, students think about questions for each section and subsection of the book as they read it. For example, in this chapter of this book, students could ask themselves "What are the proven techniques?" and "How does the basic SQ3R system work?" The question step has two main purposes. First, it takes a conscious effort to formulate and think about the questions, which prevents mindless reading. Second, the student automatically starts thinking about the information they already know that can answer the question. It gives them a background to build on as they are reading.

- In the **Read** step, students read the section and look for the answers to the questions they formulated for the section or subsection.

- In the **Recite** step, students read the section and recite, in their own words, a summary of what they have read. Putting it into their own words requires the students to understand what they have read. Students who are unable to answer the questions for the section should go back to the read step and try again.

- In the **Review** step, students go back through the chapter by reading the heading and mentally noting what information was under each heading. It gives the student a basic summary of what that  chapter was about and allows them to note whether there are any sections that they need to go back and work on some more.

The SQ3R system is a logical, step-by-step system that allows students to have a plan to follow to help them actively read the material and ingrain it in their minds instead of mindlessly looking at the words and not getting much out of the material.

Exercise: Try It

Here is a sample of what the SQ3R method might look like.

(Excerpted from *101 Businesses You Can Start With Less Than One Thousand Dollars: For Students* by Heather Shepard.)

Are You Up For Self-Employment?

Self-employment is not for everyone; you will have to decide if self-employment is the best thing for you. It is important to get feedback from your family and those closest to you. Allow them to address the concerns and thoughts they may have about your venture. Building a business takes a lot of dedication in the first year.

Considering your current role as a student, list what you specifically think you would gain from starting your own business:

_____

Starting your own business as a student offers some very specific advantages including:

- **Financial Freedom** – When you work for someone else you get paid only for the time you actually work. When you work for yourself, you make money 24 hours a day, 7 days a week, especially if you are selling on the Web.

- **Flexible Hours** – When you work for yourself you have the advantage of creating a schedule that can bend or change as necessary so you can maintain your current school schedule. You can work more during breaks and take time off for exam week.

- **Your Time, Your Training** – When you work for yourself, you decide what is important for you to know. You will earn hands on training in a variety of subjects. In a corporate job you would be limited to one job and one set of duties and responsibilities.

- **Responsibility** – As your own boss, you are responsible for the successes or disappointments you face. As it stands right now, if you are working for someone else, you are giving that person control over your situation. By taking control of your future, you have no one to blame but yourself for your difficulties. On the other hand, you have no one to praise but yourself when you create a successful and marketable business.

- **Experience** – Owning your own business will give you the experience you need to succeed in any endeavor in the future, even if your business fails.

  We have dedicated an entire chapter to self-evaluation so you can gain some insight into your personal and professional characteristics and to help you figure out the right business and the right process to take for starting your business.

Survey: There are five main points in this section and the theme of the section is about determining if the reader is up for self-employment.

Question: What are the qualities a person needs to be ready for self-employment?
How does financial freedom relate to self-employment?
How do flexible hours relate to self-employment?
How does training relate to self-employment?
How does responsibility relate to self-employment?
How does experience relate to self-employment?

Read: Students would read through the section and think about the answers to each of the questions. Some students might highlight or underline the answers or they might write notes in the margins.

What are the qualities a person needs to be ready for self-employment?
A willingness for financial freedom, a desire to have flexible hours, the ability to train for and complete many different jobs, the responsibility to face the challenges, the desire to gain experience as a business owner.

How does financial freedom relate to self-employment?
Self-employment allows the business owner to earn money at whatever rate they wish, not just for the hours they put in at a regular job.

How do flexible hours relate to self-employment?
Self-employed students and make their work schedule fit around their school schedule.

How does training relate to self-employment?
Self-employed students can train for and work in any role they want in the business, not what is dictated by a boss.

How does responsibility relate to self-employment?
Self-employed students are responsible for the successes and failures of their businesses.

How does experience relate to self-employment?
Self-employed students can gain experience to help them in the future.

Recite: Students would then recite the answers to each of the questions.

Review: Students would read through the section by looking at the headings and saying in their own words what information is under each heading.

Build Upon the System

Successful students know they need to be flexible when it comes to using proven systems and are able to meet their needs. For example, in the SQ3R system, a student may not like reciting information aloud – or may be in a library where it's not possible – so they think about the answers, write them down, or type them on the computer. Students need to take the proven techniques and mix and match the methods to fit their needs so that they are successful for them.

For example, some students take the SQ3R method and build upon it to find a method that works for them. Here are some other techniques that students have found successful when building on the SQ3R method:

- Successful students take the time to ask questions. They do this before starting to read – they think about the topic and list, or, at the minimum, think about what questions they would like answered on that topic.

- Successful students who are struggling with comprehension of the text or pulling together ideas of a section shift to questioning and summarizing after each paragraph. They then write their questions, answers, or summaries in the margins or a notebook for easy review later.

- Some successful students do not want to take the time to ask the obvious questions and prefer to summarize instead. These students often choose to make a longer summary at the end of each page or section instead of after the end of each paragraph. This is a great technique for material that is not too difficult and when concentration levels are still high enough to retain the information. Again, the summaries should be written in a notebook or the margin of the book for easy access later.

- Successful students often write the questions in the margins and underline or highlight the key words in the paragraph that answer the questions.

- Some successful students know that highlighting and underlining an entire paragraph is not useful when going back to review, so they focus on just the key words and phrases.

- Some successful students immediately try to apply the information by asking (and answering) how they can use it at the end of each section.

- Some successful students do not overlook the "why" or "how" question. This happens when the original question is answered quickly in the paragraph and there is more information. For example, if a student reading this book asked, "Why do students build upon the system?" they can find their answer quickly in the first paragraph. Asking "How" after that will help them recognize that the tips in this bulleted list give them important and useful information as well.

- Some successful students take extra action when they do not feel like they understand the text. They take time to figure out and detail exactly what they do not understand. Often, this extra effort helps them figure it out, but if it does not, they know what questions to ask when they seek help from outside sources.

- Successful students understand the importance of reflecting on what they have read and reviewed. Reflectors take the ideas a step further than memorizing them and internalize the information by thinking about it, applying it, and coming up with innovative solutions (even if hypothetical) to the problems. They jot down questions for further clarification from the professor or for things they need to go back into the reading to find.

- Successful students realize that one of the downfalls of the SQ3R method is that it does not promote curiosity within the text. Asking questions throughout the reading process promotes a proactive approach to learning, which indicates the student is thinking about and analyzing the information as he or she processes it and also indicates he or she is not simply reading to forget in a few minutes. If the student was reading about electrical circuitry and they came across a passage that stated parallel circuits are better for larger venues, the student may ask, "Why are they better?" Successful students take advantage of this curiosity and look for the answers to their natural questions as they are reading. If the student cannot find the answer in the text, it should be jotted down for further research.

Evaluate the Results

After developing and using a system, students need to evaluate how it is working for them. They can do this by comparing how the test questions related to the questions they generated, how the lecture followed the information they studied and reviewed, and how well they think they know the material a few days after studying.

Students can also mentally review the information and jot down any further questions they have about the topic to go back to the book and clarify the answers or find more information from another source.

This is important for several reasons:

- Students who do not evaluate their reading methods may be missing the mark based on how the professor is using the material.

- Reading methods may need to be slightly tweaked or altered for each class depending on the style of the textbook, how the professor handles the information in the text versus information in the lecture, and how the student feels about the subject matter of the class. Students who do not care for the material need to make an extra effort to actively read.

- No reading method is perfect all the time. There is always room for improvement, and successful students know this, so they understand there will be situations when they need to change things.

CHAPTER 7

READ WITH A PLAN: NOTE-TAKING STRATEGIES

Even with all of the previously mentioned reading tips, some students like specific methods of taking notes on what they have read so they can easily go back and review it whenever they want. Also, successful methods of note-taking while reading can increase the active learning that is taking place throughout the reading process.

Forget What You Have Been Taught (In High School)

Up until college, writing in books is considered taboo. As a college student, however, it is important to write in your books as needed. Any student who looks at a used textbook in the bookstore knows previous students have embraced this concept as well.

Useful ways to write in the book include the following:

- Underlining
- Circling

- Highlighting
- Taking notes
- Asking and answering questions
- Marking areas for further review
- Using stickers and sticky notes to mark important areas

Successful students have different systems – from the incredibly simple to the painstakingly complicated – that help them learn the best when it comes to taking notes from a text.

Beware of Used Books

Used textbooks have a certain lure in the bookstore. They are often considerably cheaper than the newer version, but this cheaper cost comes with a price:

- Markings from previous owners can be confusing and misleading – especially when a student assumes they can just skim the markings of the previous student. The biggest problem with doing this is that there is no indication of whether or not these markings and notations were successful.

- Students have different methods to get the most out of the text. One person's method may not mesh with the next; the markings of the previous owner may get in the way of the markings of the current owner.

- Used books do not always come with all the supplemental material that the new versions do. This may not be a problem for all students or for all textbooks, but active readers and note takers often like to have as much material and as many resources as possible at their disposal.

When looking for textbooks in the bookstore, students who want to get the most out of their texts should buy new or at least find used books with the least amount of markings and notations. It will cause fewer distractions when reading and studying the material.

Love the Book

Successful students care about what the material they read and study. When they get the most out of reading or studying, they love their material and make the book their own. They can do this by using their own system of notations, mark certain pages, and add sheets of notes and questions in pages they want to explore more. Any student who has seen books loved by professors has noticed questions, markings, and added notes and can see the book has been referred back to numerous times.

Some people who like to read for pleasure also like to buy

used books because they can see what others thought about while reading the book. They get a glimpse of what the reader's life was like by reading what he or she marked and notated while reading – this is especially true for fictional books.

Students who have mastered the art of notating texts often supplied with different colored pens and highlighters, sticky notes, and note paper. This way, they have all of the supplies to mark material for different reasons as well as take notes and slip them into the book near the material to which they are referring. Sticky notes are useful to mark important pages because they can stick out of the book without falling out.

Signs that successful students have properly read and studied their books:

- The spines are no longer stiff.
- The covers are worn.
- The pages are colorful.
- Fanning the book causes pages of handwritten notes to fall out.
- Sticky notes decorate the edges of the pages.
- Corners are folded and refolded to mark pages.
- Questions, answers, and comments fill the margins.
- Diagrams and sketches of graphs, charts, and concept maps appear in blank spaces.

Read First, Notate Later

It is easy for students to get carried away with marking. When a reader highlights an entire paragraph, it means they are not actively reading and thinking about what they have read.

It is important for students to read a paragraph or a section and then go back and highlight, question, mark, and think about the material. These are the processes that require notations in the text and the results of these processes will give the reader both a better understanding of the text and enough information to spark his or her memory of what was read and learned.

Students who notate to their advantage practice the following techniques:

- Stopping after every paragraph or section. They go back and question, comment on, and synthesize what they have read.
- Asking "why," "when," and "how" to determine what the main points of the text are.
- Only highlighting main points and phrases.
- Writing meaningful comments in the margins.
- Using the margins to indicate which areas need further research or explanations.
- Highlighting key words in the text. Some students use a different colored highlighter or pen to make key words stand out and then link it to the definition, explanation, and usages of the word in the text.
- Paying attention to the supplementary material in the text. After reading the paragraph or section, they go back and study the marginal comments, graphs, charts, inserts, and sidebars – whatever information the author included – and link it back to the text.

Be Specific and Selective

Students who do not know how to actively read texts or do not have a system to help them internalize the material as they are reading mark or highlight sentences and phrases throughout the text. They may take the time to write a notation, such as "important," in the margin or put an exclamation point next to important details.

While these actions are useful in the right context, they are not specific. Instead of writing "important," successful students jot down why it is important: "three reasons why people forget" or "author's definition of 'community'." These specific notations in the margins should be paired with equally specific markings in the text. The first examples should have highlighted the three reasons (not examples or explanations at this point, but the author's statement of reason). The second example is accompanied by having the key words and phrases of the definition highlighted in the text.

Being specific can also help the reader pick out what is the main point of each paragraph or section. If successful students do not allow themselves to highlight everything in the book, then they need to take the time to find out what the author thinks is most important and go with that.

It is important to avoid getting bogged down with too much information, and highlighting and notating too much in the text often makes reviewing and studying for exams difficult because students have to wade through the information to figure out which is the most important. Instead, successful students find ways to cut back on how much is highlighted in the text and still get a complete grasp of the topic:

- Successful students do not highlight information they already know. The best thing to do is to skim through a section to see if there is any additional information they did not already know and make a note of it.

- Successful students do not notate all of the author's examples. They jot down ideas of examples that relate to their lives. This helps them understand the information while reading and reviewing, and it helps them recall the information better in the future because it has been personalized and internalized.

- Successful students do not automatically highlight the information in the sidebars, margins, and charts. They take the time to go through the information as they go through the regular text and pull out the main points as needed.

Being selective does not mean being stingy. Some students make the mistake of not marking enough. Students who read entire sections of the book and find they have marked only one or two main ideas may want to go back and rethink about what is in the section. This is a sign they are not asking enough questions or asking the right questions or they have not been actively reading. If the reading was assigned, the professor may be referring back to it either during a lecture or on an exam.

Be Neat

It is frustrating for a student who spent an hour reading the material to come back the next day and not be able to decipher his or her notes. Here are some tips to help keep the books neat:

- Use pencils instead of pens so mistakes can easily be erased.
- Think carefully before highlighting or marking any of the text.
- Limit marginal notes to one sentence per paragraph, at the most.
- Write long notations on a separate sheet of paper and slip it into the book at the page it is referencing.
- Print notes instead of using cursive.

Copy onto Paper

After completing the assigned readings, successful students take the time to copy their notes and ideas from the book into their notes for a few reasons. First, copying the notes, ideas, questions, and main points from the book onto paper is a way to review the reading one more time – writing down information helps ingrain it in their minds. Second, this method of reviewing allows students to organize the information in a manner that makes sense to them, such as an outline or concept map. Finally, this step in the reading process allows students to generate personal examples and connections to the real world. Here are some things to keep in mind when copying the information from the text onto notes:

- Successful students try systems and organizational methods until they find one that works for them.

- Successful students treat this process as an important study session as opposed to busy work that needs to be done before the "real studying" can take place.

- Successful students take the time to add in their own thoughts, questions, ideas, and examples during this process because this makes the information more memorable to them.

- Successful students take the time to highlight the key words along with their definitions and explanations in their notes. One way to do this is to use the left-hand margin of the sheet to list the key words and use the body of the paper for the explanation and other information. Another method is to split the paper into three columns and put the key word or question in the left column; put the explanation, answer, or definition in the middle column; and put the examples in the right-hand column.

Make Choices

There will always be days, weeks, or semesters when the successful student cannot keep up with all of the reading for every class. When this happens, it is time to make decisions. When the reading load is too heavy to keep up, the successful student must create a hierarchy of reading:

- Successful students find out which sources are most favored by the professor. Doing this is as simple as looking through the syllabus to see which sources appear most often. These sources should always be read.

- Successful students learn to recognize how the professor refers to the reading material in class. If the professor goes over the reading material specifically, the reading can be skimmed or skipped in these classes if there is a time crunch. When choosing to skip reading assignments for classes, successful students know they need to reevaluate this decision on a regular basis to ensure the professor continues to thoroughly cover the material in class.

- Successful students know that, if need be, they can skim supplementary materials (or skip them) unless they are told the information will appear on the exam.

- Successful students realize the scheduling of their courses is the main problem and they evaluate if they need to drop a class to take at a later time. Once and a while students will inadvertently end up with classes that are all extremely reading intensive and they may be better off taking these classes in different semesters. If this is the case, students can drop a class to take later in their college career.

NOTE: Dropping classes should not become a habit or a crutch for not wanting to examine reading strategies and time management skills. It is important to make several considerations before dropping a class, such as: Is it too late to drop without getting an incomplete? Is there really no way to successfully fit in all the work for these classes? Will dropping the class put the student below a full-time status, and if so, what are the implications of this? Will there be a charge for dropping the class after a certain date? Is the class a prerequisite for classes that the student plans on taking the following semester?

Exercise: Create a System

Write down five tips you plan to try to improve your reading efficiency.

1._____

2._____

3._____

4._____

5._____

CHAPTER 8

UNDERSTANDING SUPPLEMENTARY MATERIALS

Most class readings come from the assigned textbook, but there are times when professors assign supplementary reading. This could be a chapter from a different book, a newspaper or journal article, or a website. Whatever it is, the professor sees merit in reading it, so it is important to take it seriously.

Figure Out Why It Has Been Assigned

Students sometimes get frustrated when professors assign new or unexpected readings in addition to those listed on the syllabus. One of the first things successful students do when they are assigned these readings is to ask the professor why this particular reading has been assigned. There are several reasons for this. First, knowing why it has been assigned can give the student the motivation to do the reading on top of everything else that needs to be done. The second reason is asking why the professor assigned the

reading shows the professor that the student is interested in the class – as long as the question is asked with sincere curiosity. The third reason it is important to ask about the purpose behind the reading is it gives the student an idea of what to look for when reading. Supplemental reading can be assigned for several reasons, including the following:

- To give the students greater detail on the topic.
- To highlight specific parts of the topic.
- To show varying viewpoints of the topic.
- To prompt a discussion or debate in a future class.
- To relate the class topics to real world examples.
- To give the students more background on topics.
- To spark the students' interest in other facets of the topic.
- To simplify a confusing section of the textbook.

Do Not Dismiss Reading Strategies

Successful students follow their same reading system with supplemental readings that they follow with textbook readings. Here are more tips to help students get the most from supplemental reading assignments:

- At the minimum, students need to define the author's main purpose or approach to the topic.
- Students need to keep in mind the professor's purpose in assigning the reading so they are sure to get the right types of information from it.
- Successful students make photocopies or printouts of supplemental reading whenever possible so they can refer back to it if needed. If they cannot make a photocopy or printout of the assignment, they make the most out of their notes, even if it means taking more detailed notes than they would out of their textbook.
- Supplemental readings may contain photos, charts, graphics, and other visual items on the Internet. Successful students take the time to jot down notes and information from these items as well as the readings.

◇◇◇◇◇◇◇

CHAPTER 9

GET MORE OUT OF LECTURES

M any students think that lectures are a huge waste of time, but these students often do not know the strategies necessary to get the most out of them. It is important to treat lectures seriously because professors often talk about things in the lectures that are not in the books but will be on tests. This chapter will cover the strategies successful students use before, during, and after class to help them get the information they need from the time spent in class.

Read the Chapter before the Lecture

Successful students read the assigned reading before lecture. This has many benefits for the student:

- Students who make this process a habit prevent themselves from getting behind in the reading and cramming before exams and quizzes.

- Students who do the reading before the class are prepared for surprise quizzes or activities that the professor may decide to do in class.

- Students have a background of the information about which the professor is lecturing. They know the vocabulary – or are at least familiar with it. They also have an idea of what the main points of the lecture may be so they can anticipate what they will be listening to.

Ask One Question during Each Class Period

Successful students make it a habit to ask at least one question during the class period. The key to doing this is to make sure that the questions are meaningful and related to the topic. There are many reasons why this is a great idea for students:

- Asking meaningful questions shows the professor that the student is interested in the topic and listening to the lecture.

- Professors will get to know the students who are more vocal in class better than the ones who do not ask questions or participate in discussions.

- Students who know they have to ask one question during each class period will pay more attention to what the professor is saying.

- Many students think of questions while they are listening to a lecture but do not want to ask them during the class. By taking the initiative to ask one question per class period, students can get the information they need on the spot.

- Usually, professors will leave time for questions at the end of the class or at certain points during the class. To avoid interrupting the professor, students jot down their questions in context of their notes so they do not forget what they want to ask.

Take Good Notes during Lectures

Lectures cannot be repeated, so that puts the utmost importance on writing notes down the first time. Similar to taking notes when reading, students need to ask questions while they are listening so they receive answers. This is often a difficult task for students, but here are some tips to help:

- Sketch out any graphs, charts, or other illustrations the professor shares during the lecture.

- Listen for signal words and phrases: "This is important." "This will be on the test." "There are three (or however many) main points…"

- Find a note-taking method that works. Some students prefer to outline what the professors is saying, while others like to make lists; still others like to make charts and concept maps.

- Date the notes and number the pages in case papers get mixed up. It will be easier to put them all together.

- Sit near the front of the class to force yourself to pay attention. It also helps students see visual aids and demonstrations more clearly.

- Successful students make notations where they have further questions or where they think they may have missed something important the lecturer said. This allows them to fill in the information later.

- It is OK to stay after class and ask for clarification as long as it is a direct question about a specific part of the lecture. For example, "I think I missed the third step in the writing process, could you explain it again?" is much better than saying, "I need you to go over the writing process. I think I missed something somewhere." Students who have a specific question about a part of the lecture show that they were listening and paying attention.

- Successful students come prepared with an ample amount of paper and writing tools so they are not scrambling for materials once the lecture starts.

Combine Textbook and Lecture Notes

After each lecture, successful students should take the time to go over the notes from the reading and lecture and combine them into one set of notes. There are several different methods of doing this, and again, the successful student needs to look at these methods and develop a system that meets his or her needs. There are ways to do this to streamline the notes to make studying for exams and quizzes easier.

- **Method #1:** Make a three-column sheet. In the first column, write the key word or concept. In the second column, reiterate what the text says about it. In the third column, add in what the professor said about it during the lecture.

- **Method #2:** Combine the ideas in an outline format, paying special attention to repeat material. Material that is in both the textbook and lecture will likely be on exams.

- **Method #3:** Review and reflect on the material. Review both sets of notes, and reflect on the main ideas. Students who do this make notes in their own words instead of copying from the two other examples.

- **Method #4:** Summarize the discussed topic. Students who actively read and listen to the lecture are able to summarize the material shortly after the lecture and use the summary to recall the information when they are reviewing for exams.

Beat the Lecture Blues

Lectures, especially those in lecture halls with so many students that the professor does not recognize faces or knows names, can be boring and difficult to listen to at times. Successful students have found methods to reduce the tugging desire to daydream, fall asleep, or skip the lecture:

- Successful students sit near the front – everyday.

- Successful students do not go to the lecture hungry. A healthy snack before the lecture can do wonders for helping with the attention span.

- Successful students do not schedule lectures during the times of day when they are least able to concentrate (for many students, this is late afternoon).

- Successful students introduce themselves to the professor.

Exercise: Examine What Makes Listening During Lectures Difficult and Make a Plan to Counter Act It

Fill in the following chart with your habits during lectures. Be honest:

Class: List a current class that is primarily lecture-based.

Problem: Identify a problem that prevents you from getting the most out of the lecture such as difficulty paying attention, missing important information in your notes, or not being able to anticipate where the professor is going with his or her lecture.

Tip: List one tip from this chapter that may help you solve your problem. Try the tip during the next week or two.

Evaluation: Write down how the tip worked for you and what steps you want to take in the future to help you achieve in this class.

Class	Problem	Tip	Evaluation

CASE STUDY #3: THE SKIMMER

It's almost midnight, and you have to read 50 pages for a quiz at 8 a.m. You want to sleep but have to get this done: what do you do? Skipping the readings is out of question, but getting all the reading done appears nearly impossible. There's a solution for you, although it may not be the most efficient one.

According to a recent study in the *Journal of Experimental Psychology*: Applied, students can recall more important concepts after skimming an entire text versus reading half the text at a normal, slow pace. Instead of giving up entirely, it's better to at least skim the material and focus on the main topics. However, it's still always best to read the text all the way through to retain the most information.

Skimming is a method of rapidly moving your eyes over the text with the purpose of getting only the main ideas and general overview of the content. This is only useful in three scenarios: pre-reading to get a preview of the material, reviewing a text you've already read, and quickly reading material that doesn't need much attention to detail. Other times, it's best to not cram your reading into one sitting. Skimming should be only used as a last resort.

Below is a college student's testimony about studying for exams:

"Break studying into smaller bits over a long period of time with several fun breaks and activities in between. Studying will be much more efficient and more fun to accomplish."

When you procrastinate, you set yourself up for failure. Scheduling study sessions daily is very important and avoids cramming. Instead of relying on skimming, here are some solutions to break up your reading so it doesn't overwhelm you:

- **Time yourself:** When you tackle an assigned reading, time how long it takes you to read each page or whole assignment. After you know how long much time you need to finish the assignment, then you can determine how to spread out your readings.

- **Schedule your readings:** If you're given a few days to finish your assigned reading, break down the amount of pages into sections and read them separately. This will give your mind a break and not stress you out.

- **Don't rush:** It's important to take your time. Since you've broken down the required reading into separate sections, don't feel pressured to read fast; you can take your time.

Studies from Geoffrey B. Duggan and Stephen J. Payne from the University of Bath, UK have shown that reading the text all the way through is the only way students can remember all parts of the information, not just main ideas. Professors love to use small details from the reading on quizzes or tests. Skimming in college just won't cut it; your grades will quickly suffer. But if you break your reading up, then your assigned reading won't appear as daunting.

◇◇◇◇◇◇◇◇

CHAPTER 10

RECOGNIZE THE IMPORTANCE OF CRITICAL THINKING

F or students who have never critically thought about class material, the process can be overwhelming and frightening because many students do not know what it is or how to do it. Critical thinking is not a natural ability but with a few key tips and tricks, students can train their brains to critically analyze information without consciously thinking about it.

Critical thinking, sometimes called evaluative thinking, refers to evaluating the material at hand and involves curiosity about the subject. Successful students who critically think about the information presented to them do not just accept the information as is. They think about it, question it, and try to take it one step further. This means they try to apply it, question its validity, or disprove it for the sake of understanding it better. Critical thinkers also look closely at the source to see if it is reliable or to see if it may have an underlying reason for framing the information in a certain way. All of these processes cause the successful student to better understand the information because he or she is actively using information instead of memorizing facts.

Critical thinkers have a way of thinking that sets them apart from other people. Critical thinkers are able to impartially think about all sides to an issue and apply evidence to any viewpoint. They are skilled at organizing ideas and can successfully articulate their thoughts. Critical thinkers are also logical and can explain why something is illogical or logical. This thinking system allows for recognition of probable consequences before they occur.

Understand the Importance of Lateral Thinking

Edward do Bono, an expert on thinking, defines two different types of critical thinking: lateral thinking and vertical thinking. Lateral thinking is the type of thinking that aims to broaden the knowledge base through the generation of new possibilities. Successful students use lateral thinking strategies to help them find new information as well as to examine new perspectives.

Successful students use these strategies to develop their lateral thinking skills do the following:

- Successful students read a lot. They read their course material, the newspaper, fiction, non-fiction, magazines, and whatever they can find. Reading about other people's experiences, thoughts, and opinions helps the successful student have a myriad of information from which to draw new ideas and possibilities when they are trying to broaden their knowledge about a topic.

- Successful students also feed their curiosity. Instead of skimming over information or telling themselves they will find out more later, they take the time to find the answers to their questions when they are reading their texts for class or when they are reading for pleasure.

- Successful students keep a running lists of "why" questions in a journal or elsewhere so they can go back and answer them when they have time. When students take a genuine interest in the world around them and unlock their curiosity, they find they have many questions waiting to be answered.

- Successful students are not afraid to ask new questions and try new things, such as listening to a speaker with a differing viewpoint or on a topic with which they are not familiar or by trying an activity they have never done. New activities can change the way successful students think about familiar experiences and ideas, as well as help them broaden their thinking when they encounter new ideas.

- Successful students also examine the beliefs and customs of other cultures to see how other people view familiar activities and topics – and why.

Understand the Importance of Vertical Thinking

Vertical thinking is the thinking system that makes judgments on current information. This type of thinking is what successful students use when they need to evaluate information, because it allows them to classify and sort it.

Successful students use these strategies to help them develop their vertical thinking skills:

- Successful students list the pros and cons of each possibility.

- Successful students look for other viewpoints during this evaluation process whether it is from friends, classmates, or professors.

- Successful students think about the ramifications of each possibility before implementing an option.

- Successful students seek advice from people who experienced the situation before. If they are trying to figure out what a professor's first test will be like, they seek out people who have had classes with the professor before and ask about his or her exams.

Balance Lateral and Vertical Thinking

Lateral and vertical thinking are important for successful students. They work best together. Students use lateral thinking first to generate a list of possible solutions to a problem and then move to vertical thinking to evaluate and choose the best possibility.

Here are some examples of how lateral and vertical thinking work together:

- When deciding on a topic for a paper or presentation, successful students use lateral thinking to come up with a list of possible topics that fit in the assignment's parameters and then use vertical thinking to narrow it down to the best possible topic for them.

- When answering a short answer or essay prompt on an exam, successful students take a few minutes to think about all the possible directions they may take with the answer and then use vertical thinking to narrow it down to the best possibility.

Be Aware of Assumptions

Everyone functions on a daily basis as a result of assumptions. This includes the unsaid, often not-even-thought-about assumption that people do during their normal morning routines, such as taking showers and eating breakfast, because they assume these activities are safe. It also includes the assumptions about why fellow classmates are absent from or late to class or making the assumption about what will be covered on an exam.

The first types of assumptions are harmless and also necessary to function in life. It is not possible to try to prove these types of assumptions are correct. The second type of assumptions may be better off examined. Successful students, for example, know that it is better to critically think about what the professor may include on the exam, instead of assuming it will only be information from the lecture or from the book and then find out they are grossly unprepared for the exam. The other problem with assumptions is inaccurate ones can lead to the promotion of stereotypes, prejudices, and poor decisions.

Here are some ways to help overcome common assumptions about studying and coursework:

- Successful students do not assume there are one or two possibilities they need to choose from. They make sure they ask the questions necessary to clarify exam questions and assignment parameters, for example.

- Successful students take the time to fully understand the complexity and workload required for assignments before writing them off as easy or quick projects. This allows them to schedule ample time to complete the project. They do not assume it will be a quick project based on their first glance.

- Successful students utilize their professor's office hours by going in for clarifications on class information as well as assignment directions instead of guessing or assuming they know what the professor means.

Practice Critical Thinking Skills

Successful students who understand the concepts of critical thinking take their studying a step further than those who do not understand the importance of critical thinking. Here are some ways to do this:

- Successful students take the time to find practical applications for the material as well as figure out how the same ideas can be applied to different situations as well as the ramifications of doing so.

- Successful students also take advantage of assignments by thinking about the posed problems and the possible solutions before answering with the first thought that comes to mind. They evaluate possible solutions and figure out which one is the best fit.

- Successful students practice lateral thinking, vertical thinking, and assumption examining on a regular basis until it becomes a normal part of their day. After consciously doing these things, they think critically about everything without thinking about it.

◇◇◇◇◇◇

PART III

PUTTING IT ALL TOGETHER: PROVEN TECHNIQUES FOR EXAMS

W hile the second part of this book explains what successful students do on a regular basis, there will be times that require specific preparation for exams. Keeping up with studies on a regular basis helps, but it is also important to have techniques ready for specific studying purposes. This section of the book aims to explain how to prepare for and take various types of exams with an already busy schedule and how to do it well.

PREPARE TO STUDY

uccessful students who keep up with their studies have a much easier time when it comes to preparing for exams than those students who need to cram a month's worth (or more) of information into a night or two of studying. However, it is important to realize that different types of exams require a different method of understanding and remembering the material. Because of this, successful students take the time to question the professor about what type of exam they can expect. Most professors will be candid about what types of questions they will ask. From there, successful students know how to study and prepare for the upcoming exam.

Allot Enough Time and Start Early

The general agreement is students should allot eight to ten hours of study time for each test. This number can be altered for a few reasons, however. Tests in classes that require a lot of memorization such as anatomy, geography, or foreign language will require more time. Exams that cover only one or two chapters may require less time. Students who have not kept up with daily reading assignments should allow more time to catch up before studying. The best thing for students to do is start with about 10 hours allotted and see where it gets them. Once they become accustomed to studying and if they log how long they study, they will soon be able to judge quite accurately how long it will take to study for an exam.

Ten hours sounds like an inordinately large block of time for studying, especially for students who generally spend one to three hours studying the night before a test. While they may find this method successful on most occasions (as determined by a passing grade), it can be stressful and it does not help with retaining the knowledge for future use. Successful students understand why allotting enough time and starting early are important:

- Ten hours should be broken up into four or five smaller study sessions over the course of four or five days.

- Starting early and allotting enough time allows the successful student to not only prepare study materials but also to use a variety of active studying strategies to help ensure high marks on the test.

- Successful students who start early have enough time to contact the professor when they have questions about the material, when they need extra help understanding certain concepts; or if they have a hole in their notes they are unable to fill using the textbook.

- Taking the time to actively study allows students to retain the information in long-term memory instead of only remembering enough to squeeze a decent grade out of the test and then forgetting most materials.

- Cramming can be counterproductive in classes that have comprehensive exams since all the information will need to be restudied for each comprehensive exam. Students who rely on cramming often "get by" in college instead of getting the most out of the time and money they invest in their education.

Organize the Material and Plan a Schedule

The time allotted for studying for an exam should be carefully planned. A good way to start is to figure out as much information as possible about the test. The best way to do this is to ask the professor and students who have previously  taken the class questions about the exams. This is not cheating; it is preparation. There are two important types of questions students ask when preparing for exams: questions about format and questions about content.

Questions to ask about the format:

- How many questions will be on the exam?

- What type of questions will be on the exam (essay, multiple choice, true or false, and so forth)?
- How much time will there be to complete the exam?
- Where will the testing room be? In large classes, the students may be separated into several rooms for the exam.
- Will the students be required to answer all of the questions or will there be a choice of answering only a certain number of questions?

Questions to ask about the content:

- What material will be covered on the exam?
- Is there a study guide for the exam?
- Will the professor conduct a study session for the exam?
- Are there one or two specific parts of the information that are more important to focus on?
- What supporting materials will be covered on the exam?

Once students know the above information, they can tailor their studying sessions to meet these needs. Objective exams, such as multiple-choice questions, true or false, and matching, require students to know more specific details and facts, while essay exams require students to understand broader concepts and know how they apply to situations.

When planning a study schedule, successful students start four or five days before the day of the exam. The first study session should be spent organizing the materials and the next three or four sessions should be studying the materials using a variety of study methods. Successful students have found these tips to be helpful when figuring out how and when to study:

- It is easy to get hung up on organizing and preparing study materials, so they set a time limit on this section of one or two hours. Otherwise, it is easy to put off studying by organizing, rereading, outlining, and re-outlining material instead of actively studying it.

- It is also important to view the planning and organizing stage as a valid study session, so it should not be done in front of the television or while visiting with friends. When taken seriously, the planning stage can help familiarize the student with the information.

- Students take the organization time to determine which main points need to be studied and then find notes from lectures and other materials that go with each main point.

- The planning session is a time to develop study sheets such as concept maps, note cards, questions, outlines, and tests as well as to answer the study guide questions and predict essay exam questions that will be used later in the study schedule. Active studying strategies and necessary materials will be discussed in the next chapter.

- The planning session also requires the student to block out time each day to study the materials and lists what will be studied each day. Some students like to study one section of the material each day with a final review at the end, while others prefer to study all the material using a different method each day with a final review at the end.

- Successful students realize the importance of not planning a study session immediately preceding the exam. They know it helps the brain to get ready for the exam to do something relaxing such as listening to music, visiting with friends, going for a walk, or doing anything else that is fun to give the brain time to think about the information without cramming.

Predict Questions

Every so often, students find themselves in a class where the professor gives them a list of questions that will be on the exam. Sometimes, the list is definitive in that it is a copy of the exam; other times, it is a database of questions from which the professor will pull questions for the exam, and still other times it may be a list of questions similar to the questions on the exam. Students with these resources have one important step completed for them because they know what to study. On most occasions, however, professors are not this generous, and it is important for students to predict which questions will be on the exam to help them know what to study.

An effective way to prepare the material for study sessions is to predict which questions will be on the exam. Successful students find that predicting about four or five times the number of questions that will be on the actual exam is a good number. These questions and their answers can be used to create study materials for various active studying sessions as described in the next chapter.

Before predicting questions, it is important to know what types of questions to ask. For objective tests, questions should be specific and include definitions, dates, people, key concepts, and formulas. Anything that is bold, highlighted, or in the margins of the textbook as well as main points in the lecture notes is a great place to start. Another place to find information is in the key terms at the end of the chapters and any key terms suggested during lectures. Subjective, or essay, exams focus more on general topics. These questions can be made from the main points in the lecture and textbook, but also focus on application from the questions and may require the students to tie together two or more main points. Predicted subjective questions should emulate this.

It also helps to think about the specific subject when trying to predict questions.

Math: While most objective questions on math exams will require the student to demonstrate the usage of learned formulas, there will be other objective questions relating to mathematicians and theory:

- Who first discovered…
- Why was "X" finally discounted?
- When is "X" not the best formula to use for…

Math exams may also contain subjective questions as well:

- Explain why it is it important to…
- Outline the theory behind…
- Give three examples of how "X" could be used to…

Social Sciences: These classes including history, geography, psychology, sociology, and philosophy, allow for a wide range of both objective and subjective questions. Some common types of objective questions are

- What date did…?
- Who was the first person to…?
- Why did…?
- What is…?
- The best definition of "X" is…
- Which of the following is the biggest effect of…?
- The result of "X" was…
- What do experts believe is the cause of…?
- Which happened first…?

Common subjective questions for social sciences include:

- Trace the events leading up to…
- Compare and contrast two events, people, theories, or concepts…
- Explain the causes or effects of…
- What is the relationship between…?
- Apply "X" theory to your own life…
- Explain why someone would choose "X" over "Y"…

Language: Whether the class is a foreign language or an English class, it will either focus on usage (such as vocabulary and grammar) or literature (including historical and cultural accounts).

Objective tests for language classes may include questions that ask about vocabulary, definitions, proper usage, and grammar. The questions for literature classes focus on comprehension, including key events, characters or people, the order of events, and the effects of events. Subjective tests delve further. Foreign language tests can have similar questions as social sciences about history and culture. Literature classes may ask students to:

- Analyze a certain aspect of a reading
- Compare and contrast two characters or concepts in a reading or in two separate readings
- Apply or trace events
- Explain how they would have reacted if they were a character in the story

Science: Objective questions deal with definitions, dates, theories, concepts, hypothesis, and experiments. Subjective questions may ask the students to:

- Explain a process
- Apply a hypothesis
- Compare theories
- Contrast concepts
- Trace events leading up to a discovery

Utilize Provided Resources

Many students arrive at college with the preconceived notion that they are on their own. What they do not realize is colleges and universities, while learning institutions at heart, are also "businesses" in the sense that they need to succeed to stay afloat. The best way to prove success for colleges and universities is to promote the success of their students. They know they cannot give As to every student, so they create a plethora of resources for students to help them earn successful grades.

However, these resources are not used as much as they could be. The first thing successful students do is find out what study-help resources are available to students. This can be found by visiting the Dean of Students office, the library, the advising center, or the student information office in the student union. These resources include the following:

- **Writing Centers.** English majors and English graduate students act as writing tutors staff the writing centers. Students can go to the writing center for help throughout the writing process or with a draft for review.

- **Testing Review Rooms.** Some universities have a room, often in the library, which contains files of old tests from professors. Students can find the tests from their professors and use the tests as study guides.

- **Tutor Labs.** Most universities offer tutoring labs where students can sign up for tutoring sessions in whichever subject they need. They are paired with majors and graduate students to help them through the information and are often flexible in terms of the number of meetings per week and times of the sessions.

Other, often overlooked, resources for students are those offered by the professor. Anytime a professor says, "This is important" or "This will be on the exam," he or she is giving the students a sneak peek at what information will be required for the exam. Other things professors may offer to students for help:

- **Study Sessions.** Professors often schedule a study session in the evening the night before or a few nights before an exam. Students are allowed to come with questions and often the professor will go over key concepts that will appear on the exam.

- **Study Groups.** Some professors organize study groups or set up a time and place for interested students to meet to study for an exam.

- **Study Guides.** Professors sometimes hand out study guides that list the information needed to do well on the exam. Students should study all of the information on the guide since it will likely appear on the exam.

Successful students learn how to create their own study guides using resources they often overlook. Previous assignments, review questions, and quizzes are great at helping students ascertain what will be on the exam.

Finally, successful students inquire in the library for resources for certain topics. Sometimes, the library media center has computer programs or links to Web sites that contain practice tests for entry-level general education subjects. While these practice tests may not be written specifically by the professor, if they cover the information offered in the classes, they will be helpful – if only as a review the day before the test.

CASE STUDY #4: THE CAFFEINE ADDICT

Whether it's actually a necessity or not, caffeine is the go-to source of productivity and energy when serious studying needs to happen. But like most things, some students go overboard on their caffeine intake. However, the right amount of caffeine consumption actually boosts your mental health.

According to a 2014 research study from Johns Hopkins University, caffeine does more than just serve as an energy booster—it also enhances your memory. While this is good news for college students, there are also side effects to consider when you drink too much caffeine and not stay hydrated.

Drinking more than 28 cups of coffee a week—or more than four cups a day—increases your risk of serious health problems, according to a recent study from Mayo Clinic. Watching your caffeine intake is very vital for your health. If you drink too much caffeine, you could have insomnia, feel nervous and jittery or become dehydrated. You should always drink an 8-ounce glass of water for every cup of coffee. Drinking coffee only when you study or write a paper is fine, but if you drink it constantly throughout the day, make sure you're not going overboard with it.

Below are some anonymous students' thoughts and personal experience with caffeine intake:

"I usually don't drink caffeine. On late nights at the library, I might have coffee or tea, but it's nothing so major as to keep me up all night. It's mostly just something to have. I usually drink water, and I would never take caffeine pills or any kind of energy drink."

"Sometimes, I drink coffee (4 times a month), but mostly drink tea (3-4 times a week)."

Besides coffee, college students have resorted to stronger, more potent measures of caffeine intake such as Red Bull, Monster and Rockstar. These energy drinks contain stimulants (i.e. guarana and ginseng) and have about 75 to over 200 milligrams of caffeine per drink, according to a recent health survey from Brown University.

When you consume energy drinks, you may have an increased heart rate and blood pressure, dehydration, and insomnia. These aren't the most ideal forms of caffeine intake, so it's best to stay away from them.

Drinking too many energy drinks can cause worse side effects down the road, too.

There are other alternatives to studying efficiently. If you find that you don't like coffee or how it makes you feel, then try these other methods:

- **Water:** Surprised by this solution? Most people are. A recent British Psychological Society study found that undergrads who drank water during exams outperformed those who didn't. Water helps hydrate your brain, ease away test anxiety, and improves memory. Try this method next time you sit down to write that brain-draining paper or study for that arduous exam.

- **Tea:** Although it's less popular than coffee or energy drinks, tea is extremely good for your health and can boost your memory with just one to three cups per sitting. Green tea improves memory the best, but black tea and herbal teas help keep you alert just as well. This is also a great alternative for those who hate the taste of coffee. The best teas to try are green tea and black tea, which have the most caffeine.

CHAPTER 12

ACTIVE STUDYING STRATEGIES

S imply reading and rereading notes is not enough for most students. To get to know and understand the information, successful students find active studying strategies to be the most successful. While most students find a few of these strategies that they like the best, it is also important to remember that many successful students use two or three different strategies when studying for each test to help them remember the information better and to be able to recall information more easily when under the pressure of the actual exam.

Summarize and Condense

Summarizing and condensing works for subjective exams requires students to have a general knowledge of the information and to be able to recall it and apply it, but does not require the students to remember specific dates, numbers, or definitions. Throughout this process, students put the information into their own words and restate it several times to help them understand the concepts and main points. The students continue summarizing and condensing the information until they are able to use a basic key word study sheet to help them recall information. Here is how it is done:

- Determine how many sheets are needed. The idea is to get one main point or concept on each sheet of paper. One way to determine this is to look at the syllabus to see which main points are listed. Sometimes there will be one main concept covered each day or each week. Another way is to make a sheet on each individual lecture and its accompanying reading assignment.

- List each main point or concept on the top of each sheet of paper.

- Go through all of the lecture and text notes and rewrite the appropriate information on each sheet. This can be done as a paragraph or as an outline.

One consideration for making these sheets if the test is strictly essay questions and the professor provides a list of possible essay questions is each sheet should cover one essay question. The information the student adds to the sheet should be the answer to the question.

At this point, the preparation work for this type of active studying is completed. There are several ways to use the sheets, but the basic premise is that the students read and review the sheets until they can remember enough of the information to condense it down one step. If it is a three-step outline, they can rewrite the outline leaving out the third step but still recalling the information when looking at the outline. If it is paragraph, they condense the paragraph into fewer sentences. They continue to condense the information until all they have left is a basic form of the original that still has the key words. As they review this basic sheet they can recall the details related to each key word.

Here is an example of how this works:

Original Text:

(Excerpted from *101 Businesses You Can Start With Less Than One Thousand Dollars: For Students* by Heather Shepard.)

Health Care for the Self-employed

Health care can be a major expense, especially when you are on your own. Here are some options for those just getting their business off the ground to consider.

First.   You can get free health care through your counties jobs and family service center. Your local jobs and family service centers can give you and your family full coverage insurance depending on how much your current family income is. You should contact your local jobs and family service center to find out how to apply and to see if you are eligible for this practical benefit.

Second.   You can locate a health clinic that accepts payment on a sliding scale. There are a number of clinics that use a sliding scale for the use of their services. They take into account your current income and adjust it to how much you can afford. This could come out to you paying anywhere from 0 to 100 percent. Normally these clinics are found in your local phone book. This also applies to many clinical dentist offices as well.

Third.   You can become a member of low cost health care options with your state or local government. You can contact your local health department to obtain information on local government or national government programs for working families. The benefits are unlimited and include complete dental, medical, eye, and prescription services for a low fee. Eligibility depends on your family size and current income ratio.

Fourth.   Membership groups, such as small business and the type of industry you are affiliated with (writers, media, and so on) all offer their members low cost health insurance.

One thing many hospitals do not always disclose is that you can also receive emergency visits on a sliding scale. If you have an emergency visit or are forced to have unforeseen surgery and are currently without health care, you can ask for an H-CAP application. How much you pay will be on a family size to current income ratio. This program will/could almost pay off the entire hospital bill.

Summary #1:

There are four ways to find affordable health care for self-employed business owners.

The first step is to look into the county's jobs and family service center, which will often provide insurance at a rate determined by the family's income. It requires an application and is only available to eligible families.

The second step is to look for health clinics that charge for services on a sliding scale based on the patient's or family's income. Based on the current income, people pay a percentage of the original cost of the service or treatment. This is also an option for dental care.

The third step is to look into state and local government programs for working families and often include dental, eye, and medical care. Families need to apply and be eligible for such programs.

The fourth step is to look into health insurance offered to members of professional groups. This insurance is often at a lower cost that if they purchased the insurance independently.

Summary #2:

There are four ways to find affordable health care:

1. Look for county programs through the jobs and family service center to see if the family's income makes them eligible.
2. Find health clinics that offer services on a sliding percentage scale based on the family's income.
3. Utilize state and local government programs to determine eligibility for dental, eye, and medical care programs.
4. Investigate health insurance options with professional membership groups.

Summary #3:

Four ways to find affordable health care:

1. County jobs and family services center
2. Health clinics with sliding scales
3. Local and state government programs
4. Professional membership groups

Students who use this method find different ways to implement the process:

- Some successful students like to complete one step on each study sheet during each study session.

- Some successful students prefer to complete all of the condensing steps on one or a few of the study sheets at each study session and then use a few minutes at the beginning of the next study session to review the basic remaining study sheet.

- Some successful students like to recreate the original sheet at the final review session. They take the basic sheet of keywords and rewrite either the original outline or the original paragraphs and compare it to the original study sheet to see what information they have forgotten.

Use Flashcards

Creating flashcards is a great way for students to study material for objective exams. The flashcards are portable and can be saved to use for studying and reviewing for comprehensive exams later in the semester.

Flashcards are successful study aids for all subjects. Here are some examples:

Subject	Side 1	Side 1
History	Person's Name Date Name of a Battle Name of an Era	Significance Events Details Details/description
Science	Key word Sketch Name of a process Element	Definition Description Process Description
Literature	Character Author Title Keywords Act or scene number	Description Name of works Outline of plot Definitions Outline of events
Foreign Language	Foreign word Grammar rule Verb Historical dates	English word Example Conjugation Significance

Successful students offer the following tips when using flashcards to study:

- **Make them early.** Successful students make flashcards throughout the semester so they are ready when it is time to study for an exam. One way to quicken this process is to highlight or mark key information in the notes and then go back and convert the information to the flashcard.

- **Use the space.** Successful students use both the front and back of the flashcards. One side has a key word or concept and the other side has the definition or explanation. This way they can study the information from both sides.

- **Master a few at a time.** Successful students do not overwhelm themselves with trying to master 100 flashcards in one sitting. They carry the cards with them and try to master 15 or 20 at a time. Then they move onto the next set while taking time to review the already mastered sets periodically.

- **Group them accordingly.** Successful students find a logical way to group the flash card whether it is by lecture topic or type of card (as indicated by the type of information on side one in the chart).

- **Review appropriately.** Successful students take the time to review the entire collection of flashcards one last time before the exam.

Use Visual Depictions of Information

Visual depictions can be great study aids for both subjective and objective tests. The options for these depictions include maps, timelines, charts, graphs, diagrams, and cluster maps. Similar to the two previous methods, the information on the visual depictions should be grouped by main point or concept if they are being used to cover all of the information to be studied.

The difference with visual depictions is they do not need to cover all of the information if the students use them along with another active study method. For example, a timeline may be appropriate to help a student remember the details of part of a larger event that he or she is studying. Students can also use visual depictions to help them tie the main points together such as trying to figure out how seemingly unrelated historical events led up to one significant historical event through the use of a cluster map:

Successful students use these visual depictions in many different ways to aide in their studying. They can:

- Study the visual depictions and try to recreate them.
- Use the visual depictions to help them grasp a concept and write their own version of the concept down for studying as either a summary sheet or a flash card.
- Summarize and condense the visual depictions similar to how they summarize and condense outlines and paragraphs.

- Create diagrams on the flash cards with a description on the back.
- Continually review the visual depiction.
- Be rest assured that the act of creating the visual depiction was a great study experience in and of itself.

Create a Study Group

Successful students know study groups can be one of the largest assets when it comes to study aids, but they can also be the biggest downfall for students who do not know how to use them correctly. Here are some helpful hints that successful students use to make study groups work for them:

- Jumpstart study groups. About a week before the exam, study groups can work together to predict questions and share their predictions with each other. This is a great way to streamline the process.

- End with a review session. Peers are great for reviewing as well. Use a final group review session to quiz one another and discuss the concepts the day before the exam. This is also a great time to have others help clear up misunderstandings.

- Know whom to avoid. Sometimes study groups have people who do not do any work on their own and expect to glean off of the hard workers in the group. Successful students know to excuse themselves from this group to either go study alone or find a different group.

- Balance leadership and teamwork. Study groups need to stay on task and a leader to keep them on task. The leader needs to remember, though, this is a group of peers so it is important to not become a dictator of how they spend their time.

Master the Review

Last-chance review sessions are a great asset for successful students. By this time, they have prepared their study materials and spent several study sessions actively studying the material. The last study session before the test should be a review instead of trying to cram in more new information which may stress the brain too much.

These review sessions should not occur immediately before the class, but can occur the night before or earlier in the day. There are many different ways to review. Successful students may:

- Recreate their study sheets and compare the new one with the original.
- Make one last pass through the flashcards.
- Take a self-created test using the questions predicted earlier.
- Take an old test from the test collections at the university.
- Recite information on the study sheets.
- Write out answers to possible essay questions.
- Explain visual depictions to study partners or study groups.

Whatever method successful students use, they make sure they have gone over all of the information one last time and do not use this time to try to learn new information. The review session should be proof to the students that they know the information and are prepared for the upcoming exam.

CASE STUDY #5:
YOUR TALKATIVE FRIEND(S)

Sometimes, studying with friends makes studying in general more appealing. You may feel more relaxed and plan on getting more work done with your best friend at your side. However, you may get easily distracted and lose precious studying time when your friend catches you up on his or her entire day. Studying with talkative friends is never a good idea.

Most people, and even researchers as well, have vacillating opinions on studying with friends, classmates or alone. There isn't a specific formula for studying; it's subjective and ultimately up to the student. Weighing the pros and cons of studying with friends and examining your personal study habits will determine whether or not you should study with friends, or people in general.

The cons of studying with friends include wasting time (i.e. talking), not studying as effectively, and being more prone to other distractions. Cracking down on yourself is worth it in the end. If you spend three solid hours studying for calculus, then you can spend an hour catching up with your friend or play in an intramural sport after you finish your work.

There are many pros of studying with friends and in groups than most people are aware of. Some of the positives include, but not limited to:

- **Motivation:** Your friends are some of the best motivators for you. They know your strengths, weaknesses and advice that you need to hear. They're in tune with personality and moods, so they know when you need to take a break or need to be cheered up. Studying with friends may benefit you, especially if you tend to stress out.

- **Reinforcement:** After you've been studying for awhile, you may become negative and want to quit after attempting several math problems or don't understand certain concepts for an upcoming midterm. Your friends or study group will reinforce your confidence and help you out with what you're struggling with.

- **Accountability:** According to a recent research study from Dominican University of California, people (i.e. students) who wrote down goals, shared them with a friend, and sent them weekly updates were 33 percent more successful in accomplishing their goals. Having accountability can work wonders in your life. If you schedule study sessions or study long periods with friends, they will keep you on task and make you show up to the library.

- **Commitment:** You and your friends will depend on each other to show up to study sessions and study effectively the entire time. It's harder to break a commitment, especially one with a best friend, than promise to study on your own and stick to that promise.

- **Test Each Other:** Studying with a friend allows you to talk about subjects out loud, brainstorm creative ideas, and test each other. Testing your knowledge on a subject is one of the most effective ways to study. Your friend will not only be patient with you, but will also know how to test you the best.

The solution is simple; if you're prone to distractions, then you should probably study on your own. But if you think you can benefit from studying with friends or classmates, then give it a try. Experimenting with different study scenarios will widen your studying abilities and refresh your mentality while studying.

CHAPTER 13

PLAN A TEST-TAKING STRATEGY

A ctively studying is the best way to do well on an exam, but it is also important for students to know what to do and expect when they get to the exam. For some students, exam time is a time of great anxiety to the point that, even though they know the information, they are unable to perform on the exam. Other students find themselves making careless mistakes that cost them valuable points. Successful students know great strategies can be applied to all test-taking situations to help them relax as well as stop losing points for careless reasons.

Overcome Test Anxiety

Test anxiety is not only normal but also necessary for students to take the time to prepare for the exam. If there were no anxiety, they would not feel the need to prepare for the exam. Test anxiety manifests itself into varying degrees of both physical and mental symptoms including sweating, nausea, headaches, butterflies, forgetfulness, worry, lack of concentration, and physical and mental tensing. Successful students, even those who experience extreme test anxiety, have found ways to overcome these sometimes debilitating symptoms:

- Prepare and study.

- Practice relaxation techniques such as taking deep breaths and slowly exhaling or purposefully tensing and relaxing muscles.

- Recite positive statements before and during the exam such as: "I can do this," "I am relaxed," and "I am prepared; I know t he information."

- Monitor the timing. Successful students determine if it is better to get to the exam site early or right on time. This is different for everyone because some people who arrive early get all worked up about the exam while others need that extra time to relax and focus.

- Arrive prepared. A great way to reduce test anxiety is to get to the exam room on time and well prepared. Successful students have used the restroom and dressed appropriately so they are not too cold or too warm. They also have plenty of writing utensils and paper to get them through the exam.

- Progress through the test. Some people with high test anxiety find working from the end of the test to the beginning is the best. Others skim through all of the questions and answer those they know first and then go back to do the others. Still others get overly anxious about certain types of questions such as true or false or matching so it is best to leave those sections for the end.

Resist the Urge

It happens in classrooms right before an exam. Students are talking about the information and asking each other for help or advice. They are cramming more information into their brains. Successful students resist the urge to partake in or listen to these conversations for many reasons:

- They have studied and know the information.

- They do not want to get information from other students that may not be accurate.

- They do not want to try to cram any more new information into their brains.

- They have relaxed for a while before the exam so they do not want to start working their brains until the exam starts.

Read Directions

Successful students take a few minutes to carefully look over the exam and get a feel of what is expected of them. They not only skim over the questions, but also carefully read the directions and underline or circle key words. Sometimes a test section may seem self-explanatory, but the professor may have made a few notes in the directions that, if not followed, can cost the student valuable points simply for careless errors. These directions may include:

- Choosing all of the correct answers on multiple-choice questions.

- Choosing only the incorrect answer on multiple-choice questions.

- Using all of the options on matching even if some terms have more than one answer.

- Correcting false statements on true-or-false sections.

- Only completing a certain number of questions.

Prioritize and Budget Time

Professors often only allow students the regular class time to finish an exam. Because of this, successful students have found ways to prioritize questions and budget their time to ensure they have enough time to finish the exam. They allow themselves to make a game plan for the first few minutes (no more than five) before starting to answer questions.

First of all, successful students decide which questions to do first and which ones to leave until the end:

- Some successful students go through the entire exam and answer all of the questions they know first and then go back to work on the rest.

- Some successful students complete the types of questions they like the best first and leave the types of questions they least like for last.

- Some successful students complete the questions worth the most points first and do the questions worth the least points last.

Second, successful students develop their own methods on how to budget their time. One way to stay on this time budget is to make notes on the test indicating the time they need to be done with each section.

- Some successful students set a certain amount of time per question or per page based on the number of questions per page.

- Some successful students use the formula that the percentage of points equals the percentage of time. So, if the student has 50 minutes to complete the 100-point test, each point can take 30 seconds or a five-point question can take two and a half minutes. This sounds complicated, but successful students who use this method know if all of the questions are worth two points except for the essay worth 20 points, they can spend ten minutes on the essay and 40 minutes on the rest of the test as a whole.

Successful students know if they want to make sure they finish an exam in time, they skip questions they are struggling with and go back to work on them at the end. Another benefit to doing this is that they may read a different question that will jog their memory enough to find the answer to the question they were not sure about. Other questions may also provide clues to at least rule out some possible answers and narrow down the list of possible correct answers.

Use Every Second

Successful students make sure to budget in time to review the exam before handing it in to the professor – the professor is not going to give extra points to students who finish early, so it is okay to take any extra time to review the exam.

Some students read this section and shake their heads because they are firm believers in sticking with their first instinct when it comes to answering exam questions. This is absolutely true. When reviewing a test, successful students know in the majority of cases, the only time they should change an answer is if they found information on another part of the test that led them to the correct answer.

Here are some exceptions to that rule that makes reviewing a vital step in successful exam taking:

- Successful students read the directions again to make sure they were followed accordingly.

- Successful students double check answer sheets to make sure the answers are in the correct spots.

- Successful students look for spelling, grammar, and editing errors in essays and short answers.

- Successful students spend time looking over questions that require complex answers to make sure they did not inadvertently skip a step or miss an important point.

- Successful students ask themselves if the answer makes sense in relation to the question.

CHAPTER 14

TAKE THE OBJECTIVE EXAM

One of the biggest advantages of the objective exam is that objective questions do not require the student to have total recall of the information, just the ability to recognize accurate information. The downfall for many students is they need to know the details and the offered possible answers can confuse them when the facts are hazily remembered.

Make the Right Choice

When completing multiple-choice exams, successful students develop a plan that works for them. When completing multiple-choice exams, students look over all the questions and answer the ones they know first. Then, they work on the remaining questions. Here are some hints that successful students use to help them get past the difficult questions they encounter:

Example: The first step in successfully taking an exam is to:

    A. The key words.

B.   Answer the easy questions first.

C.   Budget the time.

D.   Read the directions.

E.   All of the above.

- **Look for grammatical errors.** If the possible answer does not grammatically match up with the stem, then it can be discarded as a correct answer. For example, "A" does not grammatically fit with the stem so it can be thrown out as an option.

- **Read all possibilities.** There may be a good answer to the question and a better answer to the question. In the above example, a student may read "B" and think it is a good answer, and it is a good answer. However, "D" is the best answer because students need to read the directions before they know how to answer even the easy questions correctly.

- **Underline key words and phrases.** This helps the student focus on the details that may eliminate some possibly answers. In the above question, students should underline "first step" to help them focus on the absolute first step not just one of the first steps.

- **Make statements.** Another tip that successful students use on difficult multiple choice questions is to make the question and each possible answer into a statement and then determine if the statement is true or false. The ones they know for sure are false can be eliminated. In the above example, the statements would be:

> A. The first step in successfully taking an exam is to the key words.
>
> B. The first step in successfully taking an exam is to answer the easy questions first.
>
> C. The first step in successfully taking an exam is to budget the time.
>
> D. The first step in successfully taking an exam is to read the directions.

Choice "A" is not grammatically correct so it has been eliminated and "B" and "C" are both false and "D" is true so it is the correct choice.

- **Answer before looking.** Some successful students try to answer the question before looking at the alternatives so they do not confuse themselves with the distracters.

- **Deal with "all of the above."** This possible answer can be eliminated if there is one answer that students know for sure is wrong. Likewise, if two possible answers are right, it is likely the correct answer is "all of the above" even if the student is unsure about the remaining options. Students can apply the same logic to "none of the above" options.

- **When all else fails, guess.** Successful students know leaving a question blank is a way to get zero points, but putting an answer (any answer) in the blank, even if it is a guess, is better than nothing.

Find the Truth

True-or-false questions can stump the most successful students because they often find themselves second-guessing their first instinct. There are hints and tips to help get through these sections on tests, however.

- Successful students know the most important thing to remember for true-or-false tests is the entire statement must be true for the answer to be true. If there is one word that makes the statement false or even partially false, then the answer has to be false.

- Successful students underline key words and phrases in true-or-false statements to help them look for parts of the statement that may be false. Some examples of important key words include names, dates, numbers, places, and titles.

- Successful students are aware that absolute words such as "always," "none," "only," and "never" may render the statement false because there are often exceptions to the rule.

- Successful students are also aware the qualifying words such as "some," "usually," "often," "may," "many," and "can" often render an otherwise false statement true because it leaves rooms for exceptions.

- Successful students look for a word or an omission of a word that makes the statement false.

- Successful students correct the false statements if they have time to remind them of why they marked it false in the first place. This is a great way to show the professor why they marked the statement as they did in case there is a question of validity of the answer.

- Successful students know in the instances they have to guess, they should put "true," because professors will often make more true statements than false statements.

Play Matchmaker

Matching tests seem straightforward and easy, but they can take a turn for the worst with one wrong answer. This is because most students make their choices and cross of the used options. If one of these options is wrong, it can throw off all of the following answers or require a lot of reworking to fix mistakes. There is nothing worse for students working to finish an exam on time than having to erase all the answers and markings and start from scratch in a matching section. Successful students use the following tips to help them quickly and efficiently get through the matching sections on exams:

- Working from the side with the most words can be faster than the other way around because students have fewer words to scan through when choosing the correct "match."

- The best way to start is to make one pass through all of the options and only mark the answers the student knows with certainty. This will eliminate a number of options for the less certain options.

- Students should continue to go through and mark answers that can be made with certainty based on which options are left. The second pass through will yield a few more answers based on the eliminated options from the first time and so on for each pass through all of the remaining options.

- If students get to a point where they cannot make any more certain answers, then it is time to eliminate the possibilities that are not correct. After that, students should guess.

- Finally, it is important to do a quick read through to make sure there were no clerical errors in marking the answers.

CHAPTER 15

TAKE THE ESSAY EXAM

E ssay exams require a different type of knowledge than objective exams because essay exams often ask the student to apply the information. This means the student must have a deeper understanding of the information and how the different concepts and main points relate to one another.

Successful students know the first step in completing an essay exam is to carefully read the directions. This will tell them how many questions to answer, how long the answers should be, what extra information must be turned in such as outlines and notes, and what format the students should use such as writing only on one side of the paper or skipping lines. Successful students also know it is important to analyze the questions to make sure they have a good understanding of what is being asked. Students can read the chapter in the next section called "Understanding Directive Words" to help them decode essay exam questions.

Successful students also:

- Refrain from answering more than the assigned number of questions. This allows them to focus their energy on the number that will be graded.

- Look for clues when there is not a specified length. Essay or short answer questions that only leave one-third or one-quarter of the page are not asking for more than a few sentences for an answer. Questions that have one or more pages are looking for longer, more in-depth answers.

- Read through all of the questions before starting to answer them so they can choose the questions they are most qualified to answer.

- Plan with a short outline and few notes before writing.

- Avoid a rough draft since there is rarely time to write a final draft. Thus, they take the necessary steps to ensure proper organization and neatness the first time through.

- Do not discard their experience with the writing process. They may condense the steps, but they are all still there. This means they create a thesis statement, write an outline, and draft the essay. Then, if there is still time, they do a quick editing session to catch any major errors.

- Answer the questions instead of simply writing down all of the information they know about the topic.

- Keep the essay neat and easy to read by using margins, neat penmanship, and blue or black ink unless something else is specified in the directions. They know this is important because it makes the professor happy during the grading process.

Above all, successful students make sure they turn in a well-written piece of writing that is focused and organized.

◇◇◇◇◇◇◇◇◇

CHAPTER 16

TAKE THE
OPEN BOOK EXAM

Open book exams, a variation on the traditional essay exams, sound easy. To most students, the mention of an open book exam is a code word for them to not study for an exam. This is a grave mistake for students who are inexperienced in the practice of open book exams. Open book exams are often more difficult than traditional exams and are meant to test the students' ability to use, apply, and think about the information instead of the students' ability to memorize and repeat facts. Open book exams require critical thinking and the ability to construct and support arguments with facts and expert opinion by posing a problem while asking the student to solve it.

Preparation is key when it comes to open book exams. Students need to know where to find the facts they need to back up their arguments, opinions, and use of the key concepts discussed. A great way to study for an open book exam is to create study sheets similar to the summarizing and condensing activity. It is not as necessary memorize the information as it is to be familiar with it and know how to apply it.

Before going to an open book exam, successful students get clear notes from the professor about what they are and are not allowed to bring to the test. Some professors put no limits, while others only allow one notebook or textbook. Sometimes students may only bring in a specific number of sheets of paper filled with notes.

Open book exams can be overwhelming for students who have not experienced them, but here are some great tips for successful students:

- **Less is more.** It is possible to bring too much information into the test. The test is often timed so there is not enough time to go through piles and piles of resources. This is where preparation helps. Often, one or two textbooks and good notes are the keys to successful supplies.

- **Make a cheat sheet.** Students who are allowed to bring in their own notes find it useful to have a cheat sheet of main points, important dates, key formulas, or other relevant information for quick access during the exam.

- **Read carefully.** This includes both directions and exam questions. The directions will give information on the required format of the exam, while the questions will explain what type of information is requested. Students should refer to the "Understand Directive Words" chapter for more information on how to answer specific types of questions.

- **Quote the experts.** When answering the essay questions, successful students quote the book and other experts covered in class materials to back up their answers, but they also know the professor is not looking for an answer copied right out of the book so they include their own ideas, opinions, and analysis.

- **Put main focus on content.** Some students struggle with answering essay questions because they are perfectionists when it comes to writing. This is a difficult habit to break, but with time constraints often present in open book exams, successful students should put priority on content and worry about style later. This does not mean they need to disregard all of their writing skills; it means they do not have to write a stellar metaphor when a plain comparison does the trick. Another example is using a regular word instead of taking the time to look up the "perfect" word in a thesaurus.

- **Know when to stop.** Most open book exams are designed with limits – either page limits, time limits, or both. This means students need to be able to state their answers concisely and accurately. Successful students aim for concise, accurate, and thoughtful answers based on evidence.

There is another less common type of open book exam. These exams are take-home exams where the professor assigns questions and gives students a certain amount of time outside of class to complete the answer. These tests do not require as much preparation before the exam, but they do require a thorough use of materials to answer the posed question.

CHAPTER 17

REVIEW RETURNED TESTS

Upon leaving the classroom after an exam, most students try to forget about the exam as soon as possible. Other than looking at their grade, they ignore the scored exam. What they do not realize is they are foregoing an easy task that can be one of the most successful practices to help them improve their grade or ensure continued success on future exams in the class: Successful students take an hour or two to review all of their returned test and analyze how well their study methods worked and where the study methods failed.

Look at Mistakes

Successful students take the time to go over their mistakes. They do this for a few reasons. First, it helps them note what types of information they either did not study or studied wrong. It also helps them see if they need help mastering a certain concept before moving on to something new in the course. Looking at the mistakes also helps students see if they made careless errors or if they misread the directions. Since professors tend to find an exam style and stick with it, this review of errors will help when taking future exams. Finally, going over the mistakes helps students see what type of information the professor looks for, especially on short answers and essay questions.

- Successful students go one step further and take the time to find out and understand the correct answer. If they cannot figure out the right answer or understand why their answer was wrong, they go to the professor seeking an explanation and help in understanding the correct answer.

- Successful students also look for the right answer in notes from the text and the lectures to check their note-taking accuracy. If they strictly studied their notes and the information was wrong in the notes, then they know to do more careful note-taking in the future.

- Successful students make notes of the areas of information they missed on the exam so they know what needs to be relearned instead of just reviewed for comprehensive exams later in the semester.

Read and Understand Comments

Successful students make sure they can read and understand the comments written on the exam. If they cannot read or do not understand, they know to plan a visit to the professor for clarification. This is important because these comments often give great insight on what types of information the professor looks for and helps the students know what to include in the future:

- Comments that say, "You *might* have…" mean, "You *should* have…" or, "In the future you may try…" means, "In the future you *should* try…"

- Professors also comment on the use of details by telling when and where students need more details and when and where they need to be more general in their answers.

- They also may point out patterns in errors such as, "It looks like you might be confusing X and Y by the way you are answering these questions."

- Professors may not fully understand a student's answers and may make a request to see the student to discuss it. They will not try to track the student down to have this discussion, but will leave it up to the student to find the professor and initiate the discussion.

Professors also make comments about the format of the exam and on the students' test-taking procedures that will help the students evaluate and alter their testing strategies for the next test:

- A comment on a test that says the professor could not read the student's handwriting is a clue that the student needs to slow down and be neat.

- Comments may point out an error in how the student followed directions, and since professors tend to use the same basic format for all tests, this helps the student know what to look for in the future.

- Professors may also give the students hints on which parts of the test to focus on first if the test was not completed in the time allotted.

Professors will also write comments about the students test-taking method or obvious patterns. For essay exams, they may comment on the support or format of the answer.

Create a Study Log

Some successful students keep a study log for each class. The log includes how long they studied for the exam and their grade. Other information included in the log is:

- Whether most of the questions came from the assigned reading or from the lecture.

- What types of problems were troublesome so they can work on strategies for these types of problems.

- Comments from the professor to help the students evaluate their test-taking strategies.

- Specific parts of the information that were studied incorrectly or insufficiently.

PART IV

COMPLETING ASSIGNMENTS

While regular reading assignments, study guides, and review questions are rarely graded in college-level courses, students are often required to complete papers, presentations, or projects. Because there are few smaller assignments to go along with them, these larger assignments often make up a large percentage of a student's grade in the class, so it is important they understand the assignment and have a strategy in place to complete the assignment effectively.

◇◇◇◇◇◇◇◇

CHAPTER 18

UNDERSTAND DIRECTIVE WORDS AND PHRASES

Many students struggle with assignments because they do not understand what they are supposed to do. They often see the topic in the project description and spend their time gathering information about the topic. Then they try to cram as much information as possible into the space or time allotted. The problem is they fail to take the time to understand what the professor is asking them to do with the information.

On most occasions, professors ask the students to use the information they have researched in a specific way. This request is often in the assignment description in the form of directive words and phrases. Successful students know how to decode these directive words and phrases so they can understand what type of project they are to complete, what type of information they are to include, and what type of approach they should take with completing the project.

Take the topic of "learning styles" for example. Some students will look at a prompt and see the key words "learning styles" and write everything they know about learning styles. This is not the best approach. Successful students are aware of other key words in the assignment prompt and use them together to formulate their assignment.

Decipher Level One Directive Words

Level One directive words often require the student to give information about a specific topic. This type of project requires research for facts and rarely asks for analysis, interpretation, or opinions of the topic. Successful students approach these types of projects as if they are a reporter looking for all of the information and report "just the facts" of who, what, where, when, how, and why.

Describe. These assignments request students to write a detailed description of the topic. These assignments should follow a logical sequence and use plenty of examples to "show" the professor or audience what they are describing.

Example: Choose and describe five learning styles.

- **Keywords:** The keywords are "five" and "describe".

- **Description:** Successful students choose their topics and write about them in a way that "shows" the professor or other audience what each learning style is using examples. They may describe the characteristics of people who prefer the learning style, in what situations the learning style is useful, and in what situations the learning style has proven to be problematic.

- **Warnings:** The assignment prompt is not asking students to judge or evaluate the learning styles so the students provide an impartial description of each one.

- **Format:** Unless otherwise noted, "describe" assignments generally look for answers in paragraph form.

Research. Assignments requesting students to research a topic are telling the students to go beyond the information presented in class and found in assigned readings. The professor wants students to dig deeper to get a more thorough understanding of the topic.

Example: Research the implications of not determining and developing a preferred learning style.

- **Keywords:** The keywords are "research," "implications," and "not."

- **Description:** Successful students know they are looking for specific information about a learning style of their choice. They must look for examples that describe what happens to students who do not know their preferred learning style and how to use it to their advantage.

- **Warnings:** Some students may not carefully read the prompt and miss the "not" in the directions. Other students may spend a good portion of the assignment describing the chosen learning style, but the prompt says to write about the implications so the students should assume the audience knows what the learning styles are.

- **Format:** The format is not noted in this instance. Answers to research prompts can be listed, written in paragraph form, or diagramed. Students who are unsure should consult with the professor for further details.

State. Assignments requesting students to state the information are looking for a recollection of information. Often these prompts require brief answers with few details other than the keywords or phrases requested.

Example: State the ten learning styles discussed in class.

- **Keywords:** The keywords in this prompt are "state," "ten," and "in class."

- **Description:** Successful students know they need to think about what learning styles were presented during lectures and class discussions and to write them down.

- **Warnings:** The keyword "in class" shows students there may be different learning styles presented in the book, but the professor is looking for the ones mentioned in class. While some students may write down all of the learning styles they can think of, they need to differentiate between which ones were presented in class and which ones were presented elsewhere.

- **Format:** This prompt asks for a simple list void of details, examples, or descriptions.

Define. Assignments requesting students to define the topic are asking the students to give the topic's meaning according to someone or a specific source. Sometimes the source is specified. When it is not specified, successful students know to look for information in a few sources to find the most accurate description or definition possible.

Example: Define three learning styles based on the information given in the text.

- **Keywords:** The key words are "define," "three," "learning styles," and "text."

- **Description:** Successful students know they need to go to the text to find the information needed to complete this assignment. They look over information and devise their own definition based on what the book says.

- **Warnings:** Some students may copy the information from a source, but in most cases, the professor is looking for them to define the requested terms in their own words. Successful students know that to define a term in their own words they need to be able to fully understand it first.

- **Format:** In most instances, the prompt to define a term means the answer will be only a few sentences. There are cases, however, where the professor asks the term be defined in a longer format. In such cases, students should look for various ways to define a term including breaking the topic into smaller sections and defining each individual section.

Explain a process. Assignments requesting students to explain a process the topic are similar to the "describe" and "define" prompts. Successful students know explaining a process requires them to look at all aspects of the topic and give full details for each one and organize it in a sequential manner.

Example: Explain the process of determining a learning style.

- **Keywords:** The keywords are "explain," "process," and "learning style."

- **Description:** Successful students complete this assignment by first finding information about the steps to determine a learning style and then giving details and examples for each step.

- **Warnings:** Some students may think listing the steps is enough, but listing the steps and explaining the background, examples, and possible road blocks for each step gives more explanation than a simple, one sentence step.

- **Format:** The assignments for explain a process prompts can be written in a step-by-step list as long as the steps include explanations. Some professors may require that the information be written out in paragraph form; however, this means each step would be a paragraph in the finish project.

Enumerate/List. Assignments requesting students to enumerate or list want them to recall key words, examples, or steps in a process. These types of assignments are not looking for long explanations of the items in the list, only the basic information.

Example: List the steps a student should use to determine their learning style.

- **Keywords:** The keywords are "list," "steps," and "learning style."

- **Description:** Successful students know they need to recall, locate, or determine the steps students should take when they want to know what learning styles they prefer. They also know they do not need to describe the steps, instead list them accordingly.

- **Warnings:** Some students do not take a listing prompt seriously because it sounds easy and straightforward. For the most part, it is fairly straightforward, but students need to take the time to ensure they list all of the necessary points and do not miss anything important.

- **Format:** This assignment should be presented in a numerical list. If it is a process, the items should be listed chronologically.

Summarize. Assignments requesting students to summarize want them to take a large amount of information and condense it down into their own words. This shows the professor they understand the material enough to write it in their own words and they are able to pick out the most important points.

Example: Summarize the characteristics of three different learning styles.

- **Keywords:** The keywords are "summarize," "three," and "learning styles."

- **Description:** Successful students choose three of the given learning styles and summarize their characteristics. To do this, they pick out the main points under each one and explain them in a brief paragraph.

- **Warnings:** Some students see the word summarize and make one of two mistakes. The first mistake that some students make is copying one or more sentences from their sources that seem to describe the topic. The other common mistake for summarizers is putting the information into their own words but missing important details. Successful students know it is important to put the information into their own words and to make sure they have covered all of the main points.

- **Format:** Unless the assignment directs otherwise, a summary is written in paragraph form. Also, if there is no length requirement given in the assignment, students can gauge the length by allowing about one paragraph for each page of information that is summarized.

Diagram. Assignments requesting students to diagram want them to gather information and create a visual depiction of some sort. This diagram can be a chart, graph, timeline, cluster map, or other visual representation of the information. Sometimes the type of visual representation is specified and other times it is left up to the student to decide what will work the best.

Example: Diagram the learning styles discussed in class to highlight their shared characteristics.

- **Keywords:** The keywords are "diagram," "learning styles," and "shared characteristics."

- **Description:** Successful students know they will be able to choose which type of visual depiction they will use. They also know they need to come up with a list of characteristics for each learning style and then see which learning styles share which characteristics. There are several ways to do this. They can make a chart with the learning styles across the top and the characteristics down the side and place checkmarks in the corresponding squares to illustrate which learning styles have which characteristic. Another option is to make a cluster map that has every characteristic listed as a cluster center with the corresponding learning styles coming off of each cluster.

- **Warnings:** Some students use the same type of visual depiction time after time. This is not the most efficient way to display the information in all cases, however. For example, a timeline would not be effective in this instance.

- **Format:** The assignment format depends on the type of visual depiction chosen, but an important thing to remember regardless of the type of depiction is it should be neat and orderly. The use of colors can help highlight certain areas of the chart, but students should be careful to not make it too busy.

Trace. Assignments requesting students to trace a topic want them to show a progression through time whether it is a process, an event, or a transformation.

Example: Trace the events leading up to the discovery of learning styles.

- **Keywords:** The keywords are "trace," "up to the discovery," and "learning styles."

- **Description:** Successful students know they need to look at what prompted researchers to look into the possibility of learning styles and what they did to pinpoint the different kinds of learning styles.

- **Warnings:** Students who do not read the prompt carefully may not trace the right set of events.

- **Format:** Unless specified, there are several different ways to present this information. Prompts, such as this one, could be presented as a timeline. Other possible formats are lists, steps, and paragraphs.

Outline. Assignments requesting students to outline are instructing them to pick out the main points or key events. These assignments work well to show basic understanding of a complex theory or concept. They also work well when students need to demonstrate understanding and comprehension of reading assignments.

Example: Outline the characteristics and pros and cons of one learning style.

- **Keywords:** The keywords are "outline," "characteristics and pros and cons," and "learning style."

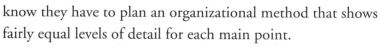

- **Description:** Successful students know they have to create a three part outline for this assignment using the three main points listed in the prompt, each with its own main points and details. They also know they have to plan an organizational method that shows fairly equal levels of detail for each main point.

- **Warnings:** Students who struggle with outlining make one of two mistakes. The first mistake is not using an organizational method. Students fail to plan out how deeply they will go into the outline and are unable to keep their organization consistent. The second mistake is giving too much detail. This type of assignment should contain the main points and essential details, but minor details should be left out of the final project.

- **Format:** This project should be presented in an outline format.

Identify. Assignments requesting students to identify are asking them to name something specific. These prompts may clarify how many items need to be identified or in what manner they should be presented.

Example: Identify in a short paragraph five methods students can use to develop their verbal learning skills.

- **Keywords:** The keywords are "identify," "paragraph," "five," and "verbal learning skills."

- **Description:** Successful students know they will need to find or recall information on verbal learning skills and write a paragraph about how students can help develop their skills. They do not need to include their opinions or justifications, but simply list the items asked for.

- **Warnings:** Some students may take the time to evaluate the merit of each of these methods, but this is not what the question is asking. Another error is not clearly reading the prompt that tells them to write the answer in paragraph form.

- **Format:** While this prompt asks for a paragraph, some identify assignments do not specify or instead, ask for a list of items.

Comment. Assignments requesting students to comment are asking them to discuss a specific portion of the topic in a clear, concise, and organized manner. The assignments assign a specific sub-topic or give a choice of sub-topics to discuss.

Example: Comment on the common struggles of visual learners in college-level classes.

- **Keywords:** The keywords are "comment," "struggles," and "visual learners."

- **Description:** Successful students know they need to write about the problems visual learners have in class.

- **Warnings:** A careless mistake with this type of prompt occurs when students fail to limit their answers to the specifications in the prompt. In this example, a mistake is not limiting answers to struggles in class. Another common mistake is when students evaluate and judge the comments instead of making the statements.

- **Format:** This prompt looks for a written answer in paragraph form. The length of the answer depends on the amount of information to be commented on. In this instance, a paragraph would suffice.

Decipher Level Two Directive Words

Level Two directive words ask the student to take the information one step further than presenting the facts in a specific manner. These types of assignments require students to interpret information and find ways

to make connections about the topic or more sub-points of the topic. Projects at this level include an equal mixture of facts and personal connections and interpretations. It is important for the students to remember, however, that all connections and interpretations should be backed by credible sources.

Discuss. Assignments requesting students to discuss the topic want them to examine the topic and talk about the validity, pros and cons, or benefits and disadvantages of the topic. Discussing a topic is showing all sides of it in an impartial manner, but it takes analyzing skills to be able to come up with and organize the information properly.

Example: There were three main benefits to determining learning styles presented during class lectures. Discuss these benefits.

- **Keywords:** The keywords are "three," "benefits," and "discuss."

- **Description:** Successful students know they need to recall the information presented in the lecture and think about the validity of each of the benefits. They state their opinions about the validity of the benefits and back them up with explanations from the lecture, other sources, and reasoning.

- **Warnings:** Discussing prompts want students to show all side of the issues so they need to take care to not write a one-sided or weighted answer to the questions.

- **Format:** The discussion is most often presented in paragraph form. In this instance, there are three paragraphs, one for each of the benefits listed.

Compare. Assignments requesting students to compare will ask them to take two or more seemingly different topics and find and discuss similarities. In some cases, the similarities are obvious and in other cases, the similarities are not obvious until the student has examined and analyzed the topics.

Example: Compare the intuitive learner with the verbal learner.

- **Keywords:** The keywords are "compare," "intuitive learner," and "verbal learner."

- **Description:** Successful students know they need to find thorough descriptions of these two types of learners and think about the characteristics for each one. They then need to draw conclusions about these characteristics to see where the similarities lie.

- **Warnings:** Some students are easily frustrated when the similarities are not readily apparent. They fail to think critically about the topics and give up without giving the assignment a chance.

- **Format:** The most common way to present this information is in paragraph form, but some students may prefer to use a Venn diagram to highlight the similarities.

Contrast. Assignments requesting students to contrast ask them to take two seemingly similar topics and highlight the differences. Similar to the compare prompts, sometimes the differences are fairly obvious and other times they are not apparent without a thorough examination of the topics.

Example: Contrast sensing learners with sequential learners.

- **Keywords:** The keywords are "contrast," "sensing learners," and "sequential learners."

- **Description:** Successful students know they need to look at the learning styles that have many similarities and think about what makes each one unique. Their finished assignment will show how, though the learning styles are similar, they have unique features.

- **Warnings:** Similar to the compare prompts, some students get frustrated when the requested information is not readily recognizable.

- **Format:** Contrast prompts result in the answers being written in paragraph form, but they can also be presented in a Venn diagram or a cluster map.

Illustrate. Assignments requesting students to illustrate are asking them to take a topic and come up with examples that show the audience the meaning of the topic. These examples can sometimes be found in lecture notes, texts, and other resources, but students who attempt to apply the topic or concept to their lives will be able to come up with unique illustrations of the topic.

Example: Illustrate the ways active learners and reflective learners can help one another.

- **Keywords:** The keywords are "illustrate," "active," "reflective," and "help."

- **Description:** Successful students know they need to look at the deficiencies of each of these types of learners and see if the advantages of the other type can fill the void in some way. They then need to connect these relationships with specific examples.

- **Warnings:** Some students stop at the point where they have made the relationships. While this is an important step, they need to go one step further to illustrate what they are saying.

- **Format:** There are several ways students can present this information. They can write the information in paragraph or essay form or they could list each way and write out the example underneath it.

Apply. Assignments requesting students to apply the topic want them to take a concept or idea and show how it can work in different settings and situations. This type of project requires thorough understanding of the topic or concept to be able to show how it will function or react in a different or real-life setting.

Example: Apply the steps for determining a learning style preference to yourself.

- **Keywords:** The keywords are "apply," "steps," "learning style," and "self."

- **Description:** Successful students know they need to take themselves through the steps to determine their individual learning style preferences. They explain how they worked through the steps and make a conclusion as to their learning style preference.

- **Warnings:** Some students may not actually apply the steps to their lives and instead go to the conclusion. While the conclusion is important, the professor uses this prompt to see that the students understood the steps in the process, not only the end result.

- **Format:** The final project is an essay that explains how the process applied to the student's situation and also highlights the results.

Cause. Assignments requesting students to discuss the causes of a topic are asking the students to explain the event or events that lead up to another event. They need to be able to look at information and figure out which events are relevant to the topic and which may be concurrent but are not directly related.

Example: Sara is a physical learner who is constantly struggling in her study skills lecture. What are some causes for her struggles?

- **Keywords:** The keywords are "physical learner," "lecture," "possible," and "causes."

- **Description:** Successful students know they have to predict possible causes based on the information they know about physical learners and the reported struggles they have in lectures.

The answer to this question is not found in the lecture notes or in the textbook, but the information leading to the answers will.

- **Warnings:** Some students may list the possible struggles that physical learners have, but if they fail to use the information to answer the question about Sara, they may lose points.

- **Format:** This type of prompt can often be answered in paragraph or list form.

Effect. Assignments requesting students to work with the effects of an event can ask the students either to discuss what happened in a real situation as a direct result of one event, or they may ask the students to predict what could happen in  a hypothetical situation using the information they already know about the topic.

Example: Mike, a visual learner, began studying with Jane, a verbal learner. What are some possible effects of this relationship for each of them?

- **Keywords:** The keywords are "visual learner," "verbal learner," "effects," and "relationship."

- **Description:** Successful students know the first thing they need to do is see how the characteristics of visual learners can balance the characteristics of verbal learners and vice versa. They know they need to form their answer by showing how the relationship will affect Mike and then how it will affect Jane.

- **Warnings:** Some students determine how verbal and visual learners can balance each other, but they fail to specify the effects for each person, thus not answering the prompt.

- **Format:** The information for this prompt can be presented in a list or a paragraph. In this instance, since there are two people, the effects could also be presented in a Venn diagram.

Relate. Assignments requesting students to relate to topics are asking them to show the connections between two or more people, events, or concepts. The assignment asks students to illustrate these relationships through examples and illustrations.

Example: Relate global learners to sequential learners.

- **Keywords:** The keywords are "relate," "global learners," and "sequential learners."

- **Description:** Successful students take time to find quality descriptions of both types of learners and look for their similarities and differences. They use the information to explain how working together would be great for them and how they would clash when working together.

- **Warnings:** Some students may write the descriptions of each type of learner and fail to make the connections on how they are related to one another.

- **Format:** These types of prompts require answer to be written in paragraph form.

Demonstrate. Assignments requesting students to demonstrate are asking them to show or prove something about the topic. Students can make this proof by using a mixture of opinions and judgments with facts, figures, and citations from experts.

Example: Demonstrate how a struggling student may use learning styles to help improve their grades.

- **Keywords:** The keywords are "demonstrate," "struggling," "learning styles," and "improve."

- **Description:** Successful students know they have to look at the process of using learning styles along the benefits of using learning styles and mesh the two to explain how struggling students can benefit. They take the information and write an essay incorporating the information with proof in the form of facts, figures, and expert opinion.

- **Warnings:** Some students discuss the benefits of using learning styles and fail to apply it to struggling students along with the process. A demonstration prompt requires students to show their knowledge and prove its validity.

- **Format:** This type of prompt requires answers to be written out in essay or paragraph form.

Decipher Level Three Directive Words

Level Three directive words require students to do the most critical thinking out of all three types. These types of assignments ask students to evaluate and apply information. A basic format for these types of assignments requires students to make a statement and defend it with facts found through research.

Review. Assignments requesting students to review want them to give a survey of the topic that praises the good points and criticizes the bad points. When students are asked to review a topic, the best thing they can do is think about a movie review and follow that format: include a quick summary, discuss the good points and bad points, then give an overall judgment.

Example: Review the use of learning styles by college students.

- **Keywords:** The keywords are "review" and "learning styles."

- **Description:** Successful students know they need to give a brief overview about the theory of learning styles, list the benefits of utilizing this theory with examples, list the disadvantages of utilizing this theory with examples, and then give an overall judgment as to whether or not they think the use of the learning styles theory is a good use of time for college students.

- **Warnings:** The review of good points and bad points should be a personal opinion backed up with expert opinion, proven examples, and logical reasoning. It should not be copied from a source.

- **Format:** Reviews are written in paragraph form.

Prove. Assignments requesting students to prove something will make a statement and then ask students to agree or disagree with it and then prove their side of the issue.

Example: Read the following statement, decide if you agree or disagree with it and then prove your side of the issue:

"Students who lean toward a verbal learning style are more likely to succeed in college than those who lean toward other learning styles."

- **Keywords:** The keywords are "read," "decide," and "prove."

- **Description:** Successful students know they need to make a decision of agreement or disagreement with the statement. Before they do so, they need to review the characteristics, advantages, and disadvantages of each type of learning style. Once they make their decision, they look for examples, expert opinion, facts, and figures to show their decision is the best decision.

- **Warnings:** A common error for students is not taking one side but instead showing the pros and cons of both sides. Another common error on this type of assignment is not giving enough solid proof of their opinion and instead restating their opinion in a variety of ways. Finally, a third common error is trying to prove their side of the issue with emotions instead of fact.

- **Format:** These assignments are written in essay or paragraph form.

Interpret. Assignments requesting students to interpret information want them to look at the information and explain its significance. Students are also expected to include their thoughts and opinions on the information and back them up with facts and logical reasoning.

Example: "A recent study found that 62 percent of students who take a learning styles mini-course during their first semester of college graduate while only 47 percent of students who do not take the mini-course during their first semester of college graduate." The students are provided with the rest of the study report including the methodology.

Interpret this study.

- **Keywords:** The keywords are "interpret" and "study."

- **Description:** Successful students know they need to read through the entire study and break it down into a few sub-topics. Once they have done that, they need to analyze the results and validity of each sub-topic. Then they draw a conclusion about the study and back it up with information, facts, and reasoning.

- **Warnings:** Some students look at the results of the study and fail to look at the methodology, process, and other provided information about the study to make their interpretation. Other students fail to include their opinions and instead restate the findings with out interpretation.

- **Format:** These assignments require the answer to be written in paragraph or essay form.

Evaluate. Assignments requesting students to evaluate want them to comment on the value of the topic. Students are expected to explain the problem, issue, or topic, and discuss the advantages and disadvantages with a final recommendation.

Example: Evaluate the process of balancing the active and reflective learner.

- **Keywords:** The keywords are "evaluate," "process," and "active and reflective learner."

- **Description:** Successful students know they first have to explain the differences of active and reflective learning. Then, they point out the problems for each type of learner if they cannot find a useful balance. They show the advantage and disadvantages of trying to strike a balance. Finally, successful students make a final recommendation on whether or not it is useful to try to strike a balance between these two learning styles.

- **Warnings:** Some students list the characteristics, advantages, and disadvantages but they fail to take the final step of including their opinions about the value of the process.

- **Format:** These assignments are completed in paragraph or essay form.

Justify. Assignments requesting students to justify give them an opportunity to develop and state an opinion about a topic. Then, the students are required to justify or prove why their opinion is valid by showing examples, expert testimony, comparisons, and reasoning.

Example: Decide whether or not you think using the theory of learning styles is an effective method to improve grades and study habits. Justify your answer.

- **Keywords:** The keywords are "learning styles," "effective," and "justify."

- **Description:** Successful students first take time to develop their opinion on the matter. Then, they look for three to four main points to support their opinion and make sure they have examples, expert testimony, comparisons, studies, and reasoning to back up their opinion. From there, they write a project that clearly states their opinion and uses a lot of sources to justify why their opinion is the best opinion.

- **Warnings:** Some students fail to use enough information to justify their opinion. The best way to overcome this obstacle is to make sure they have a variety of types of information from several sources.

- **Format:** This type of assignment is presented in paragraph or essay form.

Respond. Assignments requesting students to respond to a topic want them to state and back up their opinions. The response may be to a concept discussed in class as a whole or the professor may present a statement relating to a concept discussed in class and ask students to respond to it.

Example: Respond to the following statement:

"The best way for students to guarantee success in college is to determine their learning style and use this knowledge to their advantage."

- **Keywords:** The keywords are "respond," "guarantee," and "learning styles."

- **Description:** Successful students first spend time thinking about the statement and evaluating its validity. Once they have formed an opinion about the statement, they have to find reasons to back up this opinion. These reasons can be a variety of information including expert opinion, facts, figures, logic, or comparisons.

- **Warnings:** Some students fail to form a definitive opinion about the statement and tend to jump back and forth on both sides of the issue. Other students fail to take enough time to thoroughly back up their opinions.

- **Format:** This type of assignment is presented in paragraph or essay form.

Support or Oppose. Assignments requesting students to support or oppose want them to show the validity or invalidity of a concept or statement. The support can come in the form of examples, expert opinion, comparisons, and logical reasoning.

Example: Support or oppose the following statement:

"Students are out of luck if they have a learning style that does not meld with a professor's teaching style."

- **Keywords:** The keywords are "learning style," "teaching style," and "support or oppose."

- **Description:** Successful students know they need to decide if they want to support or oppose the statement. Then, they need to gather and use evidence that agrees with their opinion.

- **Warnings:** Some students do not completely agree or disagree with the given statements so they have a difficult time working on the project. It is important to remember they do not need to agree with what they are writing as long as they present a solid support or opposition to the statement.

- **Format:** This type of assignment is presented in paragraph or essay form.

Analyze. Assignments requesting students to analyze want them to break down the subject into sections and go over the advantages and disadvantages of each section. The project should contain an overall conclusion about the topic after each section is thoroughly reviewed.

Example: Analyze the different learning styles.

- **Keywords:** The keywords are "analyze" and "learning styles."

- **Description:** Successful students know each learning style has to be treated as a sub-topic. They have to determine the pros and cons for each learning style, describe them in the assignment, and make a final conclusion about the learning styles. This conclusion could be about learning styles as a whole, the individual learning styles, or both.

- **Warnings:** Some students list the pros and cons of the learning styles and fail to use the information to draw a conclusion. This can result in a major loss of points since the conclusion is the part of the assignment that shows the professor what the students think about the learning styles.

- **Format:** This type of assignment is presented in paragraph or essay form.

Argue. Assignments requesting students to argue want them to take a side on the issue, concept, or provided statement and prove why one side is more correct or more advantageous than the other side of the issue.

Example: Argue for or against the use of the theory of learning styles by college students.

- **Keywords:** The keywords are "argue" and "learning styles."

- **Description:** Successful students first have to decide if they think it is advantageous for students to use the theory of learning styles or not. Then, they have to determine the reasons for their opinion and gather information such as expert opinion, facts, figures, comparisons, and examples to help illustrate why their opinion is the most advantageous.

- **Warnings:** One of the biggest problems with arguing is some students fail to choose a side and jump back and forth listing the pros and cons of both sides of the issue without forming any sort of connection or conclusion.

- **Format:** This type of assignment is presented in paragraph or essay form.

Criticize. Assignments requesting students to criticize want them to make a judgment on the merit or correctness of a topic, concept, or statement. The students are expected to analyze the topic by discussing the advantages and disadvantages and using the discussions to come to an overall conclusion about the merit of the topic.

Example: Criticize the learning style theory.

- **Keywords:** The keywords are "criticize" and "learning style theory."

- **Description:** Successful students know they need to decide whether or not the learning style theory is a valuable asset to college students. Once they decide on the merit value of the theory, they show how its advantages and disadvantages support their opinion. Again, they do this through the use of expert opinion, facts, figures, comparisons, and logical reasoning.

- **Warnings:** Some students do a great job of listing the advantages and disadvantages and implying a side on the issue, but they fail to connect all the information together in a critical conclusion that shows their overall view of and answer to the prompt.

- **Format:** This type of assignment is presented in paragraph or essay form.

Handle Hybrid Directives

The previous examples show students how to approach assignment prompts that ask them to use one directive. There will be times, however, when assignment prompts will include two or more directives. The best way for students to handle these prompts is to progress through the directives starting with the level one directives then completing level two directives, and finally finishing up with the level three directives.

Here are some examples:

- List and evaluate different learning styles. A successful student first lists the learning styles and then moves on to evaluate each one according to the information on how to evaluate a topic.

- Explain and review the process of determining a learning style preference. A successful student first lists the steps in the process and then goes back and fills in the review of each step. This prompt would be well served to have a final overall review at the end as well.

- Identify three disadvantages for and explain the effects of aural learning preferences. A successful student first determines the disadvantages and then moves on to determine the overall effects of each disadvantage.

It is important for students to remember they cover all of the directives when completing the assignment so they do not lose points for the careless mistake of not following direction.

CHAPTER 19

SPECIAL CONSIDERATIONS FOR EACH TYPE OF ASSIGNMENT

There are four basic types of assignments found in college courses. While they all have similarities, each has its own special considerations. Students who understand the idiosyncrasies of each
type of assignment have a better chance of success than those who do not
take the time to understand the format of the assignment they undertake.

Research the Research Paper

Simply defined, a research paper is a paper that uses information from other sources to solve a problem. The degree of difficulty of a research paper
varies depending on which level of directives the paper uses. Most research
papers result from prompts containing level-one directives because these
directives require papers that are extremely research heavy. They contain
few, if any, personal thoughts and opinions.

Paper prompts from level-two directives are often research papers as well,
because while level two directives require more thought and analysis than
level one, they often do not require the statement of opinions. Research pa-

pers rarely result from level-three directives because these directives require the students to form and support opinions – research papers in their purest forms should be impartial accounts of the information.

There are many characteristics that help define effective research papers:

- They contain researched, sourced, and cited material. Failing to cite sources is considered plagiarism and can result not only in academic repercussions from the student's institution but could also go as far as legal action.

- They are well written. This means they contain proper language, correct grammar and mechanics, and flow well. They are also easy to read and understand without being too simplistic.

- They contain an introduction, a body, a conclusion, and a works cited page or bibliography.

Analyzing the Analysis Paper

Analysis papers are similar to research papers, but they contain more of the student's personal thoughts and opinions than research papers. Analysis papers result from level-three directives and are one-sided accounts that state the topic, explain a position on that topic, present points with support that prove the position to be correct or advantageous, and conclude with a final recommendation and reiteration of the writer's original opinion of the topic.

While analysis papers do not rely on it, students may use research to help prove their opinion about the topic. The research is often more one-sided than that found in a research paper. There will be instances when a student will not need to research for an analysis paper, however. These instances include analyses of studies where the proof will consist of reasoning and examples from the study; analyses of literary works where the proof will consist of reasoning and examples from the work; and analyses of events where the proof will consist of reasoning and examples from the event.

Presenting the Presentation

A presentation is based off of, even if indirectly, a research paper or an analysis paper. Even when the student is not directed to write the paper as a specific part of the assignment, the "paper" is the written form of the presentation. Any level of directive can prompt presentations. Regardless of this directive, however, there are important steps successful students take to help promote success with the presentation:

- Successful students write out a script for every presentation even if they only use note cards during the actual presentation.

- Successful students prepare by reading and practicing their scripts and then moving to an outline. Eventually, through many rounds of practice, students can recite their presentation using note cards containing a simple outline or key words.

- Successful students know presentations need an introduction, body, and conclusion similar to papers.

- Successful students create handouts and visual aids that enhance their material. These can be visual depictions of the material such as timelines, charts, graphs, or maps.

CHAPTER 20

ALLOW ENOUGH TIME

T here are occasions when professors announce or hand out the information for an assignment with little time to spare until the due date. This is rare, however. It is tempting for students to wait to look at the assignment sheet when they have two or three weeks until the due date and a lot of other work to complete in the meantime. This can be detrimental to students who underestimate the time it will take to complete an assignment or run into unexpected snags along the way.

Start Early

Successful students take advantage of time and start early on their assignments. This does not mean they are physically working on assignments weeks or months in advance, but they start on it in case things take longer than anticipated. If they have a clear understanding of what is expected of them for the assignment, they can spend time thinking and brainstorming before they have to sit down and work on the assignment.

The first thing they do is read through the assignment description. During this read through, they take preliminary notes and jot down any questions they may have about the assignment, the topic, or the format so that as soon as they have an opportunity to discuss the assignment with their professor, they have their questions ready.

At this point, successful students:

- Pay attention to the details, such as the length, format, and any additional materials that will need to be developed.

- Determine which citation format they will be expected to use and find the necessary information if they are not familiar with the format.

- Figure out what types of sources they are required to use and determine whether or not their resources will be readily available.

- Discuss the assignment with students who have already taken the course with the same professor to get ideas about what the professor expects on assignments.

- Set arbitrary deadlines so they can work ahead and avoid the stress of the night-before-its-due cramming session.

- Make a plan to allow at least three days for the physical writing process for the paper or practicing for a presentation.

- Write their deadlines and plan into their schedule

- Appreciate the value of thinking. Students who start early can spend a few days or weeks thinking about and analyzing the topic to help them come up more ideas.

Choose a Prompt

Sometimes an assignment sheet will give students a choice in prompts. This is a great opportunity for students because they have the chance to personalize the assignment as much as possible and, if they start early enough, they can think about their choices to pick one that interests them. Sometimes, students have a difficult time choosing a prompt. Here are some hints to help facilitate that decision:

- Students should first mark which prompt or prompts pop out to them as interesting. If nothing pops out as interesting, the students should look at it from the other perspective and cross off the prompts they are not interested in using. Either way, they have narrowed the choices.

- Students who have a difficult time choosing may take 30 minutes or an hour to come up with a topic sentence for each remaining prompt and then weigh the pros and cons of each one.

- Students who are still having difficulty can take the topic sentences to the professor and ask for advice or thoughts on what they have so far to help them eliminate more options.

Choose a Topic

Sometimes, the topic for an assignment is specified by the prompt. Other times, the prompt leaves the topic up to the student. Choosing a topic can be overwhelming and difficult, but here are some hints that successful students use when they are stumped about a topic:

- They look for a topic that interests them or for something they want to explore further.

- They take a short list of possible topics to the professor and seek advice.

- They find a topic that is fresh, new, or interesting (such as a controversial current event) and work it to fit into the assignment parameters.

- They go to the textbook and look at the case studies, asides, and examples to see if anything spurs their interest.

- They brainstorm.

- They freewrite. To freewrite, the student writes the general topic at the top of a sheet of paper. The student then sets a timer for a specific time, usually five or ten minutes. Then, the student writes whatever comes to mind. If they cannot think of anything to write, they write: "I cannot think of anything to write" until something else pops into their head. At the end of the session, the student reads through the paper to see if any good topics appeared.

- They apply the general topic to their life to see if there is any specific topic that relates.

CHAPTER 21

RESEARCH
EARLY AND EAGERLY

N ot all assignments require research, but those that do are best started early. The first step in researching for an assignment is determining if it requires research. In most cases, however, the opposite causes problems. Students assume the assignment will not require research and then are a bind the night before the due date trying to find appropriate sources. There are ways to avoid this frenzy, however, and that is by having a solid research strategy in place and ready to go for any assignment that comes along.

Avoid Cramming In Regards To Research Assignments

Students who wait to the last minute to do research often run into a variety of problems. First, the professor has given the same assignment to at least one whole section, if not more. If the assignment gives a specific topic, there will be a lot of students trying to get the same information. Successful students avoid this rush by going to the library before other students have taken a second look at the assignment sheet.

Another problem for students cramming research in at the end is there will be times when the perfect resource is at a different library and students have to wait for it to come through an intra-library loan. Depending on the library system and where the book is located, it can take anywhere from a few days to a week or two.

Finally, few professors have sympathy for students who are unable to obtain the necessary materials to complete their assignment because they waited too long to start researching. It is a shame to miss out on a successful grade due to wasted time.

Find Credible and Current Sources

It is common for students to first visit the Internet, use Google to find their assignment topic, print off a few pages, and call it a day when it comes to research. This may be OK in high school, but it is not a good way to research in college. One of the best ways to increase a chance of success is for students to make a special effort to find credible and current sources for their assignments. There are many ways to do this:

- Successful students start with general resources such as biographical encyclopedias, general encyclopedias, dictionaries, and textbooks to give them a general overview of their topic. These sources are often not the best sources to cite in the assignment, but they can be a fantastic basis to give ideas for further research.

- Successful students take the time to get a tour of the library. This gives them information about the university's online resources as well as the library's special stacks, collections, and policies. All of this information makes researching easier.

- Successful students know most professors accept websites as resources if they have credible information.

- Successful students look for a variety of information including journal articles, personal accounts, and books.

- Successful students take their topic, thesis, and found resources to the professor and ask if he or she can suggest any other resources for them to use.

Know When to Stop

It could be possible to research and research. Successful students know at some point they need to stop and move on to other parts of the assignment. The key is to stop at the right moment. This is imperative because once the student is in the writing mode of the assignment, he or she will not want to stop and go back to research more. If there is not time to go back and gather more research, the lack of information can result in weak arguments in the finished project. This is a monumental waste of time.

Here are some tips from successful students who know when to stop:

- A general rule is all main points of the final project should have two to three resources.

- Most students try to get at least two different types of sources before they quit researching.

- It is important to continue researching until all of the student's questions about the topic are answered.

- Finally, students make copies or printouts of their resources when they find them so they do not have to go back and search for the original if they missed something along the way.

Specify the Search Terms

Sometimes students have difficulty finding information for their topic and they find themselves going around in circles finding the same sources over and over again. It is frustrating on many levels for students when this happens. There are ways to prevent this frustration by carefully crafting search terms:

- Successful students create a research log to help them remember which search terms they use. This can be as simple as a list on a piece of paper to as advanced as a chart that shows certain search terms were used in which databases.

- Successful students also break down their topics to find more specific information. Instead of searching for "study skills" and hoping to find specific information on each of their main points, successful students search using keywords related to each of their main points.

- Some successful students keep a written log such as the one following to help them remember what, when, and where they have searched for information. Then whenever they use a search term, they record the information. This is also a great source for them to keep track of possible additional search terms as they think of them so they know where to start researching.

Keyword	Date	Places Used (Databases, search engines, etc)	Sources found

◇◇◇◇◇◇◇◇◇

CHAPTER 22

WRITING IS ONLY A SMALL PORTION OF THE SUCCESS

One of the biggest mistakes that students make when completing writing assignments is their failure to recognize that the actual writing part of the assignment is just a small percentage of the work necessary for a successful assignment. Successful students go through many steps and consider many options while completing their assignments. It may sound tedious or overwhelming at first, but successful students soon realize these steps and considerations soon become second nature to them and eventually writing assignments become easier.

Think about Topics in Relation to Assignments

Successful students have realized that writing assignments rarely require them to simply write down all of the information they know about a topic. When they are given a specific question to answer or writing prompt to follow, they need to carefully read the assignment, consider the directive words (see Chapter 17), and make a plan to apply the information they have found about the topic in a way that answers the question or prompt presented to them.

Example: Compare the steps in the writing process presented by the author to the writing process that you currently use.

A mistake would be to simply describe everything about the writing process. A successful student knows that he or she needs to look at the similarities and differences between their writing process and the author's writing process.

Some writing assignments are less specific and give a general topic or a type of paper and allow the students the freedom to narrow their topics from there. Especially in these cases, successful students know they need to carefully examine their topic and make sure it fits in the realm of the given assignment.

A Thesis Is A Basis

The thesis is the most important sentence in any assignment. Contrary to what most people believe, thesis statements are not just for papers. They can be an extremely useful starting point for any assignment because they help students focus their ideas and decide how to proceed. Furthermore, theses act as a roadmap to help students stay focused as they proceed through the assignment.

When writing their theses statements, successful students remember the statements need to be:

- **Concise.** Successful students know the thesis should clearly define information that they can present in the length of the assignment.

For example, a thesis that requires the reader to describe WWII is not concise enough for a five-page paper. Instead, the student would have to narrow the thesis to a specific battle, describing a specific cause, the reasons why a specific country joined the war, or the effects of the war on women in a certain part of the country.

- **General.** Successful students know the thesis should allow for enough information to be able to fill the minimum length requirements without redundancy. For example, a thesis about describing three places to research in the library probably will not provide enough information to fill a five-page paper, but it may be enough for a one-page paper.

- **Interesting and arguable.** This is especially true in instances when students have complete freedom over their topics. For example, a thesis about stating the differences between apples and oranges is not going to be interesting because most people already know the differences between apples and oranges. It also is not arguable because most people agree that apples and oranges are different. A thesis that promises to describe the similarities between apples and oranges, on the other hand, is interesting and arguable since most people will agree that the similarities are not easily seen.

- **Appropriate.** If the thesis does not follow the assignment requirements, the final paper will not follow the assignment requirements either. Successful students take a few minutes to verify that the thesis follows the assignment by turning the assignment prompt into a question and making sure the thesis answers the question.

- **Short.** Successful students try to keep their thesis statements at ten words or less. This helps them think in-depth about what they want to say and what they want to cover in their paper. While it may seem tedious to do this, it is an important planning step that will pay off immensely later in the assignment process.

Writing Process

The writing process should be used regardless of the type of assignment because it can easily apply to papers, speeches, presentation and projects. Successful students follow this writing process for all of their assignments:

Step One: Think about the assignment. Successful students read through the assignment description and start thinking about the requirements and topics before they do any physical work on the assignment. This part of the process allows them to think about possible topics as well as what angle they want to cover on the topic.

Step Two: Brainstorm and write a working outline. During this step, successful students write down all of the information they can think of about the topic as well as questions they have that will require research. Once they have brainstormed, they take the information and organize it into several main points. This is a working outline and it may be changed throughout the process. It mostly serves as a way to get started.

Brainstorming Techniques:

Successful students use a variety of brainstorming techniques to explore their topics.

Freewriting	Freewriting is a technique where the brainstormer spends a set amount of time constantly writing about the topic. When freewriting, it is important to just write and not worry about sentences, complete thoughts or grammar, spelling, or other mechanics. The important thing is to simply write whatever comes to mind regardless if it is on topic or not. If nothing comes to mind, write "I can't think of anything to write" until something else comes to mind. After the time limit, students go back and read through the writing and highlight any relevant ideas. Use these ideas as starting points for the assignment.

Listing	Listing is a brainstorming technique where the brainstormer simply lists everything he or she can think of about the topic. This can be one large list or it can be broken down into sub-topics.
Visual Depictions	Visual depictions have the brainstormer creating maps, webs, or clusters of the information about the topic. This technique starts with the topic in the middle and the information around the outside. Brainstormers can use lines and circles to connect related ideas to create the clusters or Web effect.
Cubing	Cubing is a brainstorming technique that requires the brainstormer to do six specific tasks with the topic: describe it, compare/contrast it, associate it, analyze it, apply it, and argue for or against it.
Reporting	Reporting has the brainstormer act as a reporter and look for answers to the six journalistic questions: Who? What? Where? When? Why? and How? Students who use this technique can help them get a good sense of what areas of the topic they need to research and what areas they are more familiar with.
Utilize Resources	When all other methods of brainstorming fail, students turn to the reference section at the library. Here, the dictionaries, thesaurus, and encyclopedias are great starting points to help get the ideas flowing.

Step Three: Write the thesis. At this point, students have spent time thinking and writing about the topic. Now is the time to narrow the information to one concise, arguable, and interesting thesis statement. After writing the thesis statement, students go back to the working outline to see if any of the main points needs to be changed, moved, or deleted.

Step Four: Research. Students now spend time researching the topic. Because the thesis statement sets the paper up to be both interesting and arguable, the researching stage is important for the student to find information about each of the main points to fully explain them – there should be two to three resources for each main point. If this is an assignment that does not require research, a student will then spend this time brainstorming specific ideas and information for each main point.

Step Five: Write a detailed outline. This is the stage where students read through their research, take notes, and plug the information into the working outline. It will likely involve a lot of going back and forth from notes to their research materials and their outline, but spending time on this will produce a nice, solid outline that will help in the next step immensely.

Step Six: Write. A problem for many students is that they often get distracted while writing their rough draft. The most important thing to remember is that this is a rough draft and the main idea of this step is to get the ideas on paper in a relatively organized and comprehensible manner. Successful students have found some ways to help them do this:

- Use only the outline to aid in writing to keep the focus on the writing and not additional research.
- Plan time to write the entire paper in one sitting.
- Find a quiet place with no Internet usage or other distractions.

Step Seven: Put it away. Successful students find that they can get frazzled while working on an assignment constantly. It can be helpful to write the first draft and then put it away for a couple of days. Of course, this does require planning so that they have a couple of days to do this before the assignment deadline, but most successful students will tell you it is worth it in the end because it gives them a fresh look at the assignment when they go back to finalize everything.

Step Eight: Finalize the assignment. After the assignment has "rested" for a few days, students revise it. This involves looking for grammatical errors and typos as well as the cohesiveness of ideas. This is also a great time to look for wordiness and redundancy to make the assignment as concise as possible.

At this point it is important to double-check the conclusion. Many students tend to skimp on the conclusion because they are tired of the assignment by the time they get to the end or want to rush to get it done. By putting it away for a few days, they can take a fresh look at the conclusion.

Once the assignment is finalized, students need to think about the method of how they will present the assignment to the professor:

- Double check hard copies to ensure that the printing is readable and contains all of the pages.
- Clearly label papers that will be turned in electronically.
- Practice speeches and presentations. Use visual aides during rehearsal if applicable.
- Prepare and double check audience handouts for accuracy, correctness, and proper grammar. Make sure there are enough for the size of the audience.
- Double check all projects that have multiple mediums to make sure everything is in its proper place.

Other Considerations for Projects, Papers, and Presentations

Successful students also keep in mind other considerations while completing assignments. Professors will notice the little things that make one student's assignment stand out from the rest – either for the better or for the worst. Students who follow these tips can help ensure their assignments will stand out for the better:

- **Know the Audience.** There will be times when the intended audience will be specified in the assignment prompt. When there is no specified audience, the student should complete the assignment for the students instead of the professor so they do not leave out important details that the professor may be checking for in the grading of the assignment. For example, if the students in a Child Development class are asked to make presentations about a birth defect, they will want to give information that will be beneficial to the students in the audience and not the professor, who arguably knows much of the information about the birth defects. Even though the professor will be grading the assignment, in most cases it is best to assume the audience is the class who has general knowledge of the topic but who may need background in certain areas to fully understand the information.

- **Cite Sources.** When in doubt, it is always better to cite than to not cite and end up plagiarizing something from a source. Additionally, many colleges and universities use plagiarism detection programs that help professors detect blatant copying of information. Students who are not sure about how to cite their sources should consult with their professor on the preferred citation method for the assignment.

- **Use proper grammar.** The same lingo used in e-mail and texting is not appropriate for college-level assignments.

- **Neatness and appearance can make a big impression.** Rumpled, folded, or badly printed papers do not make a good impression. All assignments that are turned in should look professional and neat to show that the student cares about the assignment and the class.

◇◇◇◇◇

PART V

HANDLING SPECIAL CIRCUMSTANCES

Colleges are always trying to keep up with new innovations to allow more students to be able to attend classes as well to provide students with the skills they will need to be competitive in the demanding world after graduation. With this in mind, college students should constantly be learning about new technology that they can incorporate into studying new material, writing essays, and exceling in the classroom in general. Below are ways to stay one step above the crowd.

◇◇◇◇◇◇◇◇◇

CHAPTER 23

UNDERSTAND ONLINE AND BLENDED CLASSES

One of the newest trends in college education is the constant incorporation of technology in the classroom. This has led to the use of online and blended classes. Blended classes often have a percentage of classes in person and the rest attend class online. Online and blended classes are great for people who cannot take traditional classes due to time constraints or location. However, online and blended classes require extra initiative from students who are willing to learn independently.

- **Participation is key.** It is not just enough to log in and read what is on the board for class. The professor needs to see your presence and participation in the class and that comes in the form of participation in the online discussions as well as questions and comments on the assignments.

- **Share your ideas.** Online classes require participation in the online discussion so students who contemplate taking an online or blended class need to be willing to participate often in the discussion boards.

- **Know the system.** Successful students take some time at the beginning of the class to get to know the system and how it works including where to find assignments, how to contact the professor directly, how to post messages, and where to post assignments.

- **Be willing to get technical help.** There will likely be times when the system is not working correctly. Successful students know it is necessary to get the technical help required to continue regular participation in the class.

- **Realize professors and classmates are real people too.** Successful students are respectful of ideas, questions, and comments posted by others.

- **Do not underestimate the need to study.** Online classes require students to study as much as, if not more than, traditional classes. Students will often find they need to use more initiative to complete the work since these classes are often extremely reading intensive.

- **Log into the class everyday.** This is the best way to find updates from the professors as well as successfully partake in the discussion. Often, online classes do not have a set time to meet and just require students participate in the discussions set forth by the professor.

- **Use proper online etiquette.**

Online Etiquette Rules

Rule	Example
Be neat and professional.	It is easy to be informal and sloppy when it comes to sending emails. There are so many abbreviations common to email and texting that it is easy to use them when responding to an online course, but this is the one way professors and fellow classmates can make an impression about one another so it is important to keep the format formal.
Be concise.	Everyone is busy and can get frustrated reading through redundant, repetitive messages. Keep everything to the point.
Stay on topic.	People like to be able to go back into the archives and quickly find a message. One way to facilitate this is to only address one topic per message.
Use an accurate "subject."	Again, so people can go back and easily find the message, keep the subject line accurate to the information in the message.
Be aware of typographical cues.	Using all caps is considered shouting and rude. Plus, it is more difficult to read that using traditional sentence case.

Rule	Example
Avoid inappropriate postings.	Students should only make class appropriate postings to an online or blended class. This is not the right venue for sharing chain letters or junk mail.
Clarify responses.	When responding to someone else's message, copy and paste the relevant section of the original message so readers can put the comments into perspective.
Respect others.	It is easy to say things online that would not be said face to face. Before hitting the send button, students should reread the messages and make sure it is appropriate. A good rule is that if they would not say it face to face they should not say it on e-mail.
Avoid humor and sarcasm.	They rarely come through in email because of the inability to convey tone of voice and facial expressions through e-mail.

In other situations, professors on traditional "live" classes may want to utilize online classroom technology to facilitate class projects or discussions to supplement the classroom work. The same tips apply even though it may be just a small percentage of the complete workload for the class.

CHAPTER 24

MASTER GROUP PROJECTS

A growing trend in college level classes is the highly dreaded group project. Most students dislike the mere thought of group projects because of all of the logistics that go into making it a success. The actual process of a group project is an important learning tool in and of itself, however, which is why professors are using this method more and more in classes: It is extremely rare for people to work completely independently in the real world. Group projects at the college level, even though sometimes extremely stressful, are great ways to practice these necessary skills. Besides, most successful students would agree that they rather make their teamwork mistakes at the college level than in the real world.

Choose the Team

There will be instances when the professor assigns groups for a project, but in many cases students are free to choose with whom they want to work with. In this case, successful students have a mental checklist of who to choose and who to avoid:

Successful students try to choose students who:

- Attend class everyday.
- Participate in class.
- Seem to get along with the professor.
- Are friendly.
- Care about school.
- Live on or near campus.
- Have similar studying habits as themselves.
- Have similar interests as themselves.

Students will eventually get to know others who are studying in the same majors and minors. This will help them determine which people may be a good fit for a group project.

Take the First Step

The group project requires that students communicate with one another. Successful students know they need to set up an initial meeting as soon as possible so they can get a start on the project. When setting up this initial meeting it is important to remember the following:

- Choose a time when everyone can meet.
- Exchange contact information including email and phone numbers.
- Make sure everyone knows where to meet.
- Delegate one person to make sure the space is available.

Be the Leader

Successful students know all groups need a leader at all times. When no one else takes the initiative to be the leader, successful students take on the role. This has many advantages:

- They can direct the project the way they see fit.
- They can make sure everyone is doing their assigned parts.
- They can keep track of progress without stepping on other members' toes.

- They can work to keep the group meetings moving swiftly to not waste anyone's time.

It is important for group leaders to not be too overbearing. Successful students know it is time to take a step back and examine the teamwork when:

- The majority of the group disagrees with how the leader is running the project.
- A section of the group members make changes without consulting the rest of the group.
- There seems to be dissent among the group members.
- Group members constantly disagree with the leader.

Delegate Tasks

The best way to delegate tasks within a group is to first find out what type of work everyone prefers doing. Successful students know it is counterproductive to ask students who prefer one type of work to do another type that they hate. The result of doing this is a group of people struggling to complete tasks they do not enjoy. Some students may be excellent at digging up obscure but important information while others are great at interviewing people for pertinent information.

When delegating tasks in group projects, successful students:

- Make a list of everything that needs to be done and check it against the assignment requirements to ensure they cover everything.
- Ask group members to choose the tasks they are most comfortable doing.
- Ensure tasks are delegated equally throughout the group.
- Invite the more shy or quiet members to share their thoughts throughout the process.

Stay on Task during Group Meetings

All groups are likely to get off-task at times, but it is especially likely to happen when two or more of the group members are friends outside of the group. They will start talking, and before the group knows it, they have wasted time getting nothing accomplished.

Other students like to complain so they will often try to make the group work session into a grievance group. Successful students know this is heading down a rough road for several reasons. First of all, it is a waste of time. Second of all, generally these complaints tend to revolve around the class, other students in the class, or the professor and participating in the complaints may get back to the person and put the student in an uncomfortable situation. Finally, complaining can be stressful, and successful students know it is important to focus on the positive.

Getting off task can be extremely frustrating for students who have other work to complete or who have other commitments after the group meeting. Students continually wasting time can cause unnecessary conflict in the group.

Successful students have a few statements they can choose from to get the group on task:

- "I have to meet another group in 30 minutes, and I'd really like to finish up so that I don't leave you with more work to do."

- "You know, it's not fair to talk about someone who isn't here."

- "I know that you guys want to make plans for this weekend, but we have to get this done tonight because I'm not going to be able to meet with you this weekend."

- "Let's talk about what is done compared to what we need to finish."

- "I just thought of something…" and then explain the new idea.

Set Deadlines

Group projects often require multi-step processes that require some things to be completed before the group can move on to other parts of the assignment. Because of this, the group needs to set specific deadlines and hold the members responsible for meeting them. Simply saying "We need to get A, B, and C done before we can do D, E, and F" is not enough to make sure everyone has time to get their work done. Consider the following when setting deadlines for tasks:

- If one of the group members cannot meet the first deadline because of the workload from other classes, assign that group member tasks from the second deadline instead.

- Make the deadlines reasonable by allowing enough time to make revisions but without requiring group members to drop everything else to complete this project.

- Whenever possible, set the deadlines so group members can complete the work at an even pace throughout the project. This will prevent the need for cramming it in right before the deadline.

Resolve Conflict

There will be conflict and disagreement anytime more than one person works on the same project. The success of the group depends on how they handle these instances of conflict and disagreement. The conflict can arise for many different reasons from not agreeing on how to proceed with the project to disagreeing on the details to include in the project. Other disagreements arise when it seems one or more students are not pulling their weight of the workload. Successful students find ways to hand the conflict before there is a total breakdown in the group.

- **Be patient.** Sometimes students need a little extra time to think things through or get their thoughts in order before they can be productive members of a group.

- **Be respectful.** It is important to remember that every member of the group is busy and sometimes there are extenuating circumstances that cause them to not work up to the par that other group members have set.

- **Be flexible.** Successful students know sometimes group members are going to have an unexpected conflict that causes them to need help getting their part of the project done. A great way to handle this is to be flexible in the deadlines or in the delegation of tasks.

- **Make a compromise.** Sometimes the best way to resolve a conflict is to make a compromise so that everyone gets a little bit of what they want. It is better to do this than to foster unrest in the group to the point of not being able to successfully complete the assignment.

- **Let it go.** There will be times that successful students need to just suck it up and do it someone else's way. Many times, one way is not better over the other in the grand scheme of things, but simply different.

- **Agree to disagree.** Other times, a disagreement about how to handle situations can go on and on. This is an unproductive waste of time for the group. If it is possible to move on with the group work without coming to an agreement, this would be great time to agree to disagree on the topic.

- **Consult the professor.** In cases where it seems impossible to work out a conflict, such as a group member consistently not showing up for meetings or consistently doing sub-par work, it may be necessary to discuss the issues with the professor. This should not be a meeting where the grieving group members complain constantly about the slacking student. Instead, the group members and the grievance should set up an appointment and outline what has happened and ask for advice on how to handle the situation. It will be most productive to have evidence and to be non-accusatory during this meeting.

- **Give accurate evaluations.** In some assignments, group members will be asked to evaluate the others in the group. At this time, it is important to give accurate statements about each student so the professor can get a clear sense of how well the group worked together.

- **Make choices.** Successful students know that if there is a student who they cannot seem to work well with for whatever reason, they try at all costs to avoid working together in groups again.

Pick up the Slack

There will be times that a successful student needs to make a difficult decision. Should they do someone else's delegated tasks or risk getting a bad grade? The simple answer is that the student should pick up the slack to protect his or her own grade. The complicated answer is that picking up the slack can be a source of contention among group members who may feel like the student picking up the slack is too controlling and not allowing them a chance to do their work. Also, if it is apparent to the professor that only one student did all the work, there may be a deduction in points if part of the assignment requirements had to do with process of working together.

CHAPTER 25

BALANCE EXTRACURRICULAR AND CURRICULAR ACTIVITIES

One of the best parts of college is becoming involved in an extracurricular activity. Extracurricular activities are school-sponsored organizations such as student government, athletics, academic clubs and organizations, service groups, and multicultural groups. Depending on the organization, time commitment can be as little as an hour or two each month to as much as 10 or more hours per week. Students who partake in extracurricular activities find they have to do some fancy scheduling and make an extra effort to get everything done, but most will agree it is worth the effort. Extracurricular activities not only foster a sense of school pride, but they also teach real world skills, enhance experiences, develop self-awareness, and look great on a resume.

Avoid Procrastinating

When it comes to participating in extracurricular activities, students find that one of the biggest downfalls is procrastination. They have so much to do that there is not time to waste time. The best way to avoid this is to stick to a study schedule as well as to schedule free time so it does not get overlook in the way of "all the other stuff."

Make a List of Priorities

Students who are successful at balancing extracurricular and curricular activities clearly know their priorities and are able to make quick decisions based on these priorities. For example, a student athlete puts her sport as one of her top priorities. To be able to continue competing she knows that she needs to keep up with her grades. This helps her overcome distractions when she is supposed to be studying. Another student may be on the student government. He knows he needs to stay healthy to be able to function well. During busy weeks, it is easy for him to say no to his normal workout in lieu of something else, but he knows if he does he will feel crummy by the end of the day and will be less productive. So, the priority of feeling healthy helps him keep his scheduled workout.

Get a Tutor

Students who are involved in time-consuming extracurricular activities do not have time to mess around. Their participation in the activity relies on getting the grade and if they are struggling in a class or think they may struggle in a subject, in which they often have difficulties, they need to explore the tutoring options offered at the university. Universities often have a variety of tutoring options from a one-time thing to regular once a week or more sessions. This scheduled tutoring time ensures the students will get the help they need when they need it instead of spending precious time struggling with the topic on their own.

Utilize University Enforced Study Sessions

Extracurricular activities that are time consuming, such as sports, often have team or university enforced study sessions. Students are required to attend, but of course no one can actually make them sit down and productively study. Successful students use this time to their advantage to study. They make sure they come prepared with a variety of work and get down to business so that when the session is over they can take a break and reward themselves for a job well done.

◇◇◇◇◇◇◇◇

CHAPTER 26

BALANCE WORK AND SCHOOL

W hile it would be nice if every college student said, "school comes first and my job is secondary", this is not the case for everyone. Some students have families to support and others simply could not afford their tuition and expenses if they did not also have a job, so it is fair to say that, in some cases, school and the job go hand-in-hand.

Regardless of why they have a job, many students think it would be ideal to be able to attend college without having to have a job. Others have found that having a job helps them stay on task when they are studying and use their scheduled work times as a motivator to get things done when they have the time. Either way, students who have jobs need to take extra care to balance it with their schoolwork.

Look on On-Campus Jobs

One way successful students balance school and work is to look for jobs on campus. These jobs are often more flexible than other jobs, and sometimes the hours can fit in between classes throughout the day. Plus, students who work on campus do not waste time commuting to a job elsewhere. There are many types of jobs available to students on most campuses:

- Food service
- Grounds keepers
- Security guards
- Libraries
- Janitorial services
- Professor and program assistants
- Department aides
- Fitness centers

- Day care centers
- Computer labs
- IT services
- Printing and copying centers
- Bookstores
- Residence halls
- Research assistants
- Tutoring

Stay Organized to Study Anywhere

Successful students who work while going to school know they need to be prepared to study during any spare time. This could be on the bus on the way to work, at work if it is slow, or during a spare 15 minutes when a lecture was let out early. To do this, successful students carry study materials with them.

Successful students also need to know where they are going to be and what they need to do. This requires them to keep a detailed schedule of work, classes, and study sessions. Successful working students also know they need to schedule free time so that they do not become burned out from constantly working.

Cut Back as Needed

Even the most organized student will need to cut back working hours at certain times of the semester to be able to be successful in the classroom. Midterms and finals, if they fall in close proximity in the same class, are often stressful weeks for every student, and those who work will want to discuss this with their employers about switching hours or taking time off to allow for the most studying time possible.

CHAPTER 27

SURVIVE FINALS WEEK

Finals week is often bittersweet for most students. Yes, it is a sign that the semester is over and students are that much closer to graduation or vacation, but finals week can induce high stress and low tolerance levels for many students. It does not need to be this way. Successful students know if they have kept up with their studies all semester. They have kept their materials, study guides, study sheets, and returned assignments organized and stayed on a regular routine that involves healthy eating and exercise. Finals week will be much less stressful than it is for those students who need to cram a few weeks', or worse, a whole semester's worth of work into the last two weeks of the semester.

Adjust Schedule

Successful students know they need to start preparation for finals week very early. The first step to preparing is to adjust your schedule to accommodate final exams as well as due dates for projects, papers, and presentations. Successful students make a two-week calendar that covers the final two weeks of the semester. Then they write in all exams and due dates for these two weeks. They also add in classes and other non-negotiable commitments. Next, they figure out how much time they will need to study for each exam and start filling in the study blocks. One important note is that they should avoid starting studying more than one week in advance of the exam because they will likely forget some of the material first studied.

Here are some other hints to reduce the stress of these last two weeks of the semester:

- Take time off of work – this may need to be approved further in advance than two weeks.

- Avoid skipping one class to study for another – students who do this may miss important information about the upcoming exam.

- Prioritize items that can be finished more than a week ahead of time, such as papers and other written assignments, to leave the week before the exams open for studying.

- This is the one time during a semester that students may need to forfeit large quantities of free time. While it is important to take breaks and relax once and a while, a movie night may not be possible until after exams.

Attend Study Sessions

Adjusting their schedule for successful students means they consider the study sessions offered by professors. These invaluable resources are overlooked by students because they do not have the time to attend the meeting. What they do not realize, however, is they will likely get valuable insight about the exam simply by attending. Professors tend to be more candid about the format of the exam to students who take the effort to attend the study sessions. For example, the professor may give details such as how many essay questions will appear or the point values of each section of the test. Even if the professor is not more candid about the exam at the study session, students who attend get a ready-made review, which can only prepare them.

Successful students take these study sessions seriously. They arrive prepared and ready to review:

- They always study first so they have a basis for the information covered and can follow information provided. Studying first also allows them to test themselves when other students ask questions.

- They arrive with a few questions of their own. Even if they do not get the chance to ask the questions, they have them ready in case no one else covers these specific topics.

- They arrive on time since professors will often start with a prepared lecture that gives the condensed version of what will be on the exam before opening the session up for questions from the students.

Stay Healthy

With all of the extra work that goes into finals week, students often look for ways to squeeze more time into the day. One of the biggest mistakes that students make when looking for ways to find more study time is to skip meals or regular workouts in lieu of studying. This is actually counterproductive, however, because it can throw the body's system out of whack when its normal routine is disrupted. Instead, successful students put staying healthy at the top of their priority list. They:

- Eat healthy, balanced meals everyday even if it means taking a little extra time to do so. Students who do not partake in a university food program may want to plan ahead and make up some meals that can be frozen in individual servings so they can pop them in the microwave instead of cooking an entire meal.

- Continue their normal exercise routine. It gives them the energy needed to make it through the day.

- Get plenty of sleep. A tired brain cannot function efficiently.

- Use exercise as a way to take a break. Instead of plopping down to watch television or surf the Internet for 20 minutes (and most students will agree that these break usually end up lasting more than 20 minutes), they go for a walk or get up and stretch.

- Pack healthy snacks and water for their study sessions so they are less tempted to binge on candy and other junk food.

Avoid Stress

Finals week can be stressful enough without the added stress of non-school related things. Successful students do their best to set aside these other distractions before they begin their finals week studying and testing schedule.

- They ask family and significant others to be flexible and understanding about their busy weeks.

- They take care of financial obligations such as paying bills before finals week starts.

- They do a major cleaning of their dorm or apartment before starting their finals studying and testing schedule so they are not stressed about a messy home or tempted to clean instead of work.

- They take plenty of breaks to clear their minds and get rejuvenated before starting another study session.

- They plan a reward at the end of finals week so they have something to look forward to during the week.

- They ask questions about their upcoming finals beforehand to get a better idea of the format of the test, the information that will be covered, and if there is a study guide available.

Stay Organized

Successful students can often attribute their success at least to staying organized even when they are busy. When they stay organized all semester, they do not have to scramble at the last minute to find materials, recreate study sheets, and fill in missing notes. Instead, they have all of the information they need ready to go when it is time to study. They also:

- Plan ahead by making a list of the materials that will be needed for each class's exam and getting them all together.

- Take the time each night to gather the needed materials for exams and study sessions the next day.

- Plan to vary study materials by studying for several exams each day.

Remember Studying and Test-Taking Strategies

Successful students remember that in the grand scheme of things, a final exam is just another test and that if they apply their normal studying and test taking strategies, they will be doing the best they can and that is, after all, all they can do. Students can use their test taking strategies along with the knowledge they have built up about the professor's testing style (from tests previous in the semester) to tailor their study sessions and prepare each individual testing strategy.

CHAPTER 28

STUDY ABROAD

Studying abroad is a fantastic opportunity for so many students that it should hardly be overlooked by anyone who wants to get the most out of his or her college career. Study abroad programs have so many benefits for students regardless of their majors and there are now so many options for lengths and types of programs that it is possible for students to be able to fit a program into their college schedules.

Understand the Benefit

Students who choose to study abroad get more than the college credits they earn while abroad. Probably the biggest benefit is the travel and ability to meet new people. It also looks great on a resume. Successful students who have studied abroad also like that they were able to:

- **Learn a new language or practice a second language.** Students who want to learn a new language find that full submersion into a country that speaks the language is the best way to become fluent.
- **Learn about different cultures including customs and foods.** Many study abroad programs also allow the students to live with

a family in the country, which gives them first-hand experience about the people and customs of the country.

- **Increase their independence and confidence.** Surviving in a completely new environment has a great effect on self-confidence!

- **Better appreciate their home country.** Students who study abroad will soon be able to identify the comforts of home that they miss the most – even those who are not necessarily homesick.

- **Understand the skills needed to function in a global economy.** Students are often offered the opportunity to participate in an internship or volunteer position so that they can see first hand how their business or area of study differs from that at home.

Additionally, students who study abroad en-roll in classes that make use of the place they are visiting. Studying European architecture is much more meaningful when the student can look at the examples first hand instead of just looking at photographs.

Choose a Program

There are so many different types of study abroad programs that it is difficult to know where to even start. Some involve one concentrated class for three weeks between semesters, others are for a few months in the summer and others are for a complete, full-load semester or year in a select location. It is important to start this search early on in college, however, so students have time to apply and complete any prerequisites necessary before embarking on their journey.

There are generally four different types of academic programs that students can choose. The first type is a full semester or year when the students go to the destination and take a full load of credits. The second type of program is the concentrated class where a professor will often take one-class worth of students to a location that is relevant to the class. They will complete the coursework as well as do supplementary activities relating to the location during a break in the semesters usually for two or three weeks. The third type of program is a summer program where the students may take a lighter load of classes and may spend more time participating in an internship or volunteer position at the same time.

The first place to look for a study abroad program is at your university. Often, the Dean of Students office or academic advisors can lead students in the right direction. If the college or university does not have their own study abroad program, then they have often partnered up with another school that does have one, and the credits will likely transfer back to the original school without a problem. Other places to look for information is on the Internet.

Students who have successfully chosen a study abroad program suggest looking at the following characteristics when choosing a program. Students should:

- Inquire about credit transfer to ensure beforehand they will get credit for all of the classes they take.
- Look at the course offerings to make sure they will have enough classes that interest them and that fit into their major.
- Find out who teaches the classes – professors from the United States who are also participating in the program or foreign professors. Both options have their pros and cons, so it is up to the student to decide whom they would prefer.
- Find out what kind of housing is available and where it will be in proximity to the location of the classes.
- Find out about cost including tuition, living expenses and extra fees.

Other considerations for choosing a program include the destination, duration of the trip, and when the program is available. Some programs require a certain number of undergraduate credits before students can apply for the program so this is also an important consideration.

Above all, it is extremely important to talk to students who have been through the program to get a first-hand view of the strengths and weaknesses of the program.

Make it Count

The biggest mistake students make with their study abroad programs is they do not capitalize on the opportunity as much as they should. There are many ways to do this.

First of all, students should thoroughly research their destination before they go so they know where they want to visit while they are there. This can be done with a travel book, on the Internet, or by talking to people who have been there.

Second of all, students should do as much as possible while there to immerse themselves in the customs and traditions of the location – they should try to frequent the places where "locals" go instead of tourists.

Finally, students need to use this opportunity to their advantage when they return home. They can do this by:

- Visiting an academic advisor to schedule classes for the upcoming semester at home. Successful students consider the classes they took during the study abroad program so they can avoid taking similar classes again.
- Seeing a career counselor at the university to help them distinguish the study abroad experience on their resume.
- Mentoring students who are deciding whether or not they want to study abroad and help them choose a program that is right for them.

PART VI

AVOIDING STUDYING DOWNFALLS: HOW TO KEEP UP WITH IT ALL

E ven the most successful, studious, and conscientious students will find themselves in situations that require extra help. There will be semesters that require obscene amounts of writing because of the mix of classes and there will be semesters that require tons of reading because of the mix of classes. There will also be semesters that are difficult because all of the classes are extremely demanding. When this happens, all students, even the most successful students, need to know what to do to survive and succeed.

CHAPTER 29

UTILIZE OFFERED RESOURCES

U niversities want their students to succeed, so they have a wide variety of resources available for students to help them. While they "advertise" many of these resources, it is not feasible for the university to tell the students about every resource available to them should they possibly need it in the future. This leaves it up to the students to investigate on their own to find the resources that will best suit their needs.

Get Involved with Academic Departments

Successful students are extremely involved with their major and minor departments. They attend department functions, join the academic organizations, and apply for the academic honor societies. This allows them to get to know the professors as well as other students in the department in a setting other than class. This is beneficial for the successful student in many ways:

- Students get to know the professor, which helps them choose which classes they want to take in the future.

- Professors get to know the students and may be more flexible or understanding when the student needs assistance.
- Students can ask other students in the department for advice on interesting classes, suggestions for certain types of projects, and help getting through specific classes.
- Professors are more likely to share information about "hidden" resources to students they know on a more personal level.
- Students will have the opportunities to help plan and choose department-sponsored events.

Frequent Tutoring and Writing Centers

Successful students know there is nothing wrong with getting help when they need it. This is why they know where to find both the tutoring center and the writing center. These centers can assist them on a one-time basis or the students can set up a regular session throughout the semester. Successful students like these opportunities because:

- It is always beneficial to get an opinion from a "fresh set of eyes" when writing a paper.

- Tutors can help students detect errors that they did not realize they were making.
- It is beneficial to be able to talk through a problem with someone who knows what they are doing.
- These services can give them the extra edge needed to stand out in class.
- These services are often free for registered students.

Students who need extra help and who are not sure where to look should consult their professors for ideas for tutors and other student aid services.

Look for Old Test Resources

At many universities, there is an invaluable resource that often goes unnoticed to many students. It is a compilation of old tests submitted by professors. These resources may be found in the library or they may be found in department offices and lounges for use by the students. They are beneficial because the students can use these tests to see what types of tests the professor writes including the format, types of questions, and level of detail. The other huge benefit is that these tests may be able to serve as study guides or practice tests for the students. When using these resources, however, students should:

- Ask the professor if his or her submitted tests are still relevant to the class because sometimes professor completely revamp their class and they end up covering different material or covering it in a different way than previous semesters.

- Avoid relying solely on these tests as a study guide because they may not cover all of the information needed to succeed on current tests.

- Avoid looking at tests for the same class from different professors since it probably will not be useful to them unless the course has a universal test for all sections.

- Realize that even if the professor has not submitted tests for their specific course, they may be able to benefit by looking at other tests submitted by the professor to get a sense of their testing style.

Find out about Study Aids on the Internet

There are so many websites on the Internet that offer free resource material and even helpful videos on YouTube. Explore these free study aids. They could help you improve your grade on your final exam.

Visit Counseling Centers

Counseling centers are useful for students. Universities will sometimes have one counseling center with different departments within or they will have several different counseling centers including general counseling, study skill counseling, financial counseling, and career counseling. Counseling centers are not just for students who need help with personal or emotional problems. Successful students have found that counseling centers can help with:

- Time management and organization
- Career choices and preparation
- Conflict resolution (between roommates or friends)
- Test anxiety
- Learning disabilities
- Financial concerns
- Peer assistance groups
- Substance abuse
- Crisis assistance
- Adjustment issues
- Multicultural issues
- Stress management
- Couple and relationship issues

Read Professor Evaluations

One of the greatest assets college students have is the ability, in most cases, to choose their schedule down to which professor they take, especially in general education classes that have multiple sections. Successful students like this because they can find professors that teach to their preferred learning style. One way that they can find professors is by looking at the university-sponsored professor evaluations, which often contain student comments about the professor and the class.

Learn How to Access Databases for Research

Successful students take advantage of these resources by getting a tour of the library or media center by a media specialist. These databases can range from general research tools to subject specific databases. With the advances in technology, these databases are usually offered on the Internet for student use outside of the library as well.

Search for Specialty Libraries and Collections

While universities usually have well-known main libraries, there may also be specialty libraries or collections that are not as well publicized. These specialty libraries and collections may be student resource rooms within an academic department or they may be housed in rooms or offices within academic or administrative buildings on campus. Successful students locate these by asking or by taking time to wander campus and taking note of potentially useful resources they find.

Use Disability Services

Successful students with disabilities often access services to help them in needed areas. Students who wish to use these services usually need to apply and be accepted to the disability services programs. After this, they will often meet with a program counselor so they can decide which support services are necessary and available. In some cases, students with temporary injuries may also be able to access these services during their recovery.

These resources often include:

- Books on tape or reading services
- Sign language or captioning services
- Classroom modifications
- Testing modifications
- Counseling
- Document conversion
- Tutoring services
- Access assistance

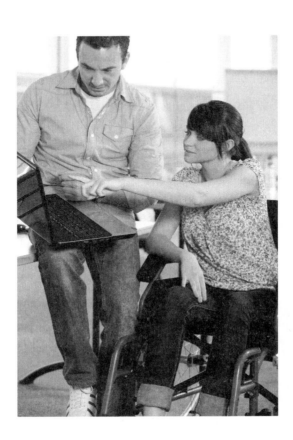

CHAPTER 30

USE FIRST YEAR TO PREPARE FOR REST

Successful students know they need to make the most of their freshman year to prepare for future classes, which becomes more difficult and demanding as they go along. There are many things first-year students can do, from scheduling to taking an afternoon to explore the campus that will help them succeed in the future.

Take a Writing Class

Any college student or graduate will say that college requires a lot of writing in different styles and formats. Students who are skilled writers and comfortable with the process will fare much better than those who are not. While it may sound overwhelming, students should ask around to find the most demanding writing professor and take that class the first year. The writing skills acquired at this point will be indispensable for the next three-plus years of college.

Believe it or not, there are many, many college students who do not know the basics of writing a good paper and those who can write well will definitely stand out to their professors in a positive way. The best ways to do this is start early with a college-level writing class and continue to use the skills learned in this class throughout their college careers.

Take a Speech Class

The same is true for a speech class. So many students suffer stage fright to the point that they dread the mere thought of taking a speech class. The truth is, however, they will be required in the vast majority of their classes to make a speech or presentation, whether formal or informal, practiced or impromptu, and the sooner they learn how to do it, the better they will fare when these assignments arise.

There is nothing worse for a student than knowing what he or she wants to say but being unable to get their point across clearly because he or she neither knows how to prepare a speech nor how to present it effectively. As with writing, speaking well comes with practice and the best way to start is in a class where they expect mistakes and will give tips and tricks to help avoid them in the future.

Take a Tour of Campus with an Upperclassman

Successful students have taken the time to find an upper-class student to take them around campus and share their knowledge about resources, social destinations, professors, majors, extra-curricular activities, shortcuts, and places to avoid. This will help the first-year student get better acclimated with the campus as soon as possible, which will help ease the transition to this new lifestyle as much as possible.

This tour can be with a resident hall advisor, an older friend, or someone from the student's intended major department. It may also be a member of a group or organization that the new student wants to join.

This tour is also a great time for the new student to ask questions about which professors to take and which ones to avoid. The upper-class student may also share information about campus safety and tips on what the new student can do to increase his or her safety on campus.

CHAPTER 31

KEEP IT REAL

C ollege can be so overwhelming for students that they may soon find themselves doing what needs to be done to get by. This is all right once and a while to get through stressful times, but students who constantly have to do this may find they are not staying true to what they want or how they want to be. Because college is a time of growing and maturing as much as it is a time of learning and earning a degree, successful students have taken the time to make sure they stay true to themselves.

Examine Values

Successful students periodically take the time to examine their values. This could be as simple as making sure they are spending enough time with their friends and family to as drastic as making sure they are being honest in their work. By examining their values, successful students help themselves stay true to their priorities – this helps them stay motivated because they know they are on the right track.

One way they examine their values is by looking at their lives to make sure they have their priorities in order and if they are not, they need to make changes to their daily lives. They can also evaluate if what they are doing is making them happy. If it is not, they need to figure out what they need to make them happy and do their best to add that to their lives.

Define Personal Success

Successful students also need to define for themselves at what point they will be successful. For some, it is earning straight A's in college and graduating with high honors. For others, personal success is earning their degree but also completing a certain type of volunteer work. Other students may deem themselves successful if they have made an impact on the campus or student body while in school. Personal success is different for everyone and those who define it for themselves will be able to judge whether or not they are successful students.

Make Goals

Many students avoid setting goals because they do not know what they want out of college or they do not know how to set goals or they simply get too overwhelmed with the idea of setting goals and then having to stick to them. It is important for students to remember, however, that goals can be modified or scrapped as their lives change. It is just important to get them set to get something to work toward and have an end in sight.

- Goals help with motivation because they give the students an end point to work toward.

- Goals help students make difficult decisions. If the decision hinders progress toward an important goal, it is probably the wrong decision.

- Goals help students with their priorities. Again, if something hinders progress toward a goal, it most likely should not be high on the priority list.

Setting goals can be overwhelming, but here are a few tips successful students use when setting goals:

- The goal needs to be desirable to the student. Too often, students set goals because they sound good or they think they will make others happy. These goals will often fall by the wayside and will often not be big motivators if the student does not want to reach them anyway.

- The goal needs to be achieved in connection with other goals. For example, a full-time student who has one goal of graduating in four years will likely not be able to fulfill a goal that requires him or her to work a full forty-hour week as well. These two items are not compatible with one another.

- The goals should be positive and explain what the students want to do, not avoid.

- The goals should be specific so the students will know when they reach them.

- The goals should be written down on paper and kept visible such as on a bulletin board or on a homepage on the Internet.

Stay Connected to Reality

Students who live and work on campus can easily lose sight of the real world. It is easy to work, study, and go to class without really paying attention to what is going on in the real world unless a professor brings up a current event. Successful students make an effort to read the newspaper, current event magazines, news sites on the Internet, or watch news programs at least once a week to keep in touch with what is happening in the world around them. If nothing else, keeping in touch with current events will help them apply the concepts they learn in class to current events, not just what is happening on campus.

Examine Majors and Minors Frequently

Students often start college with an idea of what they want to do when they are finished. The number of students who actually finish with their first major is quite low. It is not unusual for students to change majors, decide on a double major, or add an extra minor during their education. I think most students would agree it is better to add an extra semester of schooling to change a major than to finish with a degree they do not want to use. Successful students know to look for the following signs that they may be in the wrong major:

- They are making the best of the situation because they are not enjoying what they are studying.

- They do not enjoy many – or any – of their classes in their majors.

- They cannot decide on a job that they would both be qualified for and enjoy.

- They tried an internship and were miserable.

- They do not feel challenged.

- They complain about their studies, a lot.

- They feel like fellow classmates are much more interested in the subject matter than they are.

- Their priorities have changed and the current major no longer helps them work toward meeting their goals.

Know When to Transfer

It is not unusual for students to transfer from one university to another to finish their schooling. There are many reasons for the transfer including being closer to home, being at the same school as a significant other, finding a school that has a better program for the intended major, or simply wanting a change of scenery. Successful students know how to recognize the signs that they need to transfer to a different school:

- A different school has a more prestigious program for their intended major.

- The only reason the student is not changing majors is that the current school does not offer the intended major.

- The current school is becoming unaffordable.

There are also reasons why a college transfer is not necessarily the best choice. Students who are having a difficult time adjusting to college life may think it will be easier at a different school when sometimes what they just need to give it a little time. Also, students may be looking at transferring to a new school to be closer to friends. While this is not necessarily a bad idea, it could be if the new school does not have the right program for the student.

Once the decision to transfer has been made, for whatever reason, it is important the student takes his or her time so he or she can be sure to find the right school.

CHAPTER 32

◇◇◇◇◇◇◇◇

BOOST YOUR CONCENTRATION

I t happens at the worst times, even for successful students: concentration levels tend to drop when students need it most, usually the day before a big exam or when they need to finish an assignment for class. There are ways, however, that students can give their concentration a boost.

Keep a List

Probably the biggest reason why students have difficulty concentrating is that they start thinking about all of the other things they need to do as well. This could be what they need to get at the grocery store or ideas for their next project. It could also be about who they need to email and why. Successful students have found that when their minds start wandering when they need to be studying or when they are sitting in class, the best thing for them to do is to keep a notebook handy so they can make a list of whatever is trying to take over their thoughts. If they keep thinking about the grocery store, they quickly make a list. If they keep thinking about that email, then they make a list of who they want to email when they are done. That way, they know the list is waiting for them and they can stop thinking about it.

Diagnose Which Classes Cause the Most Concentration Problems

Sometimes, it is certain classes that cause concentration problems, whether during the actual class or not. While students cannot change the time of their class, they can adjust their schedule to help with in-class concentration. If the class is at the time of day when the student tends to be tired, the student can try taking a quick walk or having a light, healthy snack to give them an extra boost of energy during the class. If the class is at the end of a particularly long day, the student can try taking a break from studies and other schoolwork before the class.

If the class is causing concentration problems while studying, the student can do several things to help boost his or her concentration during study blocks. First of all, the student should plan to study for this class when he or she has the most energy. Second, the student should try to study for the class in short increments and take short, frequent breaks. Finally, the student may want to look into joining a study group for the class to try to study the material more actively.

Remove External Distractions

Another common cause of a lack of concentration is the external distractions that can often pull the student's attention away from the subject. Students who sit near a door may get distracted by noise in the hallway, or students sitting near windows may get distracted by the outdoors. Some students even sitting in the back of the class may get distracted by other students in class. So what's the solution? Successful students sit in the front of the class, especially in courses that tend to challenge their concentration.

External distractions while studying can be household chores, roommates, television, and the Internet. Students can avoid these by not studying at home and staying away from the Internet. They can also look for quiet places to study that do not have a lot of traffic that could potentially add another distraction.

Avoid Multi-Tasking

Reading and walking on the treadmill may sound like a great idea, but students who do this do not retain as much from their reading and do not get as much as they should out of their workout. Multi-tasking sounds like a great concept, but those who multitask may get more done, but not done as well as if they had concentrated on just one task at a time.

Set Mini-Goals When Concentration is at Its Worst

Students who have a difficult time concentrating may also want to try setting mini-goals to help them get their work accomplished. Here is how it works:

- A mini-goal should be able to be accomplished in a relatively short amount of time (10 to 15 minutes).

- It should be specific. "Read more for the next few minutes" is not specific. "Read the next section in the chapter and answer the relevant questions on the study guide" is extremely specific.

- There should be a reward. Take a break, have a snack, check e-mail, or chat with a friend. The reward should be quick as well so the student can get back on task for the next mini-goal.

A whole series of mini-goals will accomplish more than simply saying "I need to read this entire chapter" and daydreaming the whole time.

When All Else Fails...

Take a break. The lack of concentration is the student's brain telling him or her that it needs a break, so at this point it is a better use of time for the student to give in and do something else for a while.

IMPROVE MEMORY

There will be classes that require memorization for the test. While it is tempting for students to do the minimum to get a decent grade, it is necessary to look at why the class requires memorization. These classes are often prerequisites for other classes for a major or minor because the information memorized in the class will be applied in later classes. Examples include anatomy and physiology for pre-med students or grammar for English majors. This is the reason successful students know that remembering things just long enough to get the information onto the test paper is not always enough. This is when students take action to actively improve their memory.

Make a Conscious Effort

One way to improve memory is to make a conscious effort to do so. Students who tell themselves "I need to remember this" or "I have a good memory, it will be okay" actually trick themselves into remembering things they may not have remembered before. Simply the act of telling the brain that this is important enough to remember gives the brain a cue to help recall the information when it is necessary.

The key to this is that it works best for incidental items such as finding the car keys, remembering phone numbers and addresses, and noting a specific date. While this is not necessarily going to help a student remember all of the information for a test, it is a start and that is important as well.

Exercise the Brain

Your brain will function better if it is exercised on a regular basis. College students may argue that their brains are exercised enough as it is, but it does not hurt to participate in some fun once and a while. Successful students know that working on word, logic, and number puzzles helps to keep the brain working and improves memory overall as well.

Repeat and Recite

One of the best ways to remember things is to practice the repeat and recite method. This can be practiced with little things such as a grocery list or a list of supplies in the student's backpack. Practicing with incidental items will help the student be able to use the repeat and recite method while studying.

For studying, students can use flash cards and other active studying strategies, but they should be working in an area where they can physically speak the information to help them remember it.

Create Acronyms

Students who are trying to remember a specific list or words, the steps to a procedure, or the specific theory can use acronyms. Acronyms take the first letter of each word (or important word) and create a word or short phrase out of the initials. Once students have studied the acronym a few times, they will remember the words that go with each initial. Here are some examples:

- **F.A.C.E.:** This can help music students remember the spaces on the treble staff. Once they know this, they can fill in the notes for the lines as well.
- **H.O.M.E.S.:** The names of the Great Lakes: Huron, Ontario, Michigan, Erie, and Superior.

- **N.E.W.S.:** The directions on a compass: North, East, South, and West.
- **ROY G BIV:** The colors of the rainbow: Red, Orange, Yellow, Green, Blue, Indigo, and Violet.

Visualize the Information

Students who can put an outrageous or silly visual with the information will be able to remember the information through the visualization. For example, when trying to remember the capitol of Pennsylvania, a student may make the visualization of a big, hairy pen and think of the sentence, My HARR-y PENN is BiG to help them remember Harrisburg, Pennsylvania.

Another example of this theory is associating a person's name with his or her appearance. It helps people recall other people's names and can be successful as long as they do not share their associations with the named person since their outrageousness may be taken the wrong way.

This principal can be applied to any topic, but it works best when the students have to associate information with a key word or phrase such as a date and its events or a person and his or her significance. As long as the picture is outrageous enough to stand out in the student's memory and has enough clues to be associated with the right key words, it will be a great way to help remember the clues. The downfall is that it takes time to come up with visualizations, but this skill becomes easier with practice.

Write Sentences

Writing sentences can help students remember things in two ways. First, if students need to remember how to spell a particularly difficult word, then they could make a sentence using each of the letters as a first letter for the words in the sentence. Once they remember the sentence, they will be able to spell the word.

- **WORD:** We Only Read Dictionaries.
- **DICTIONARY:** Did I Count The Ice On Nanna's Old Road Yet?
- **FELLOW:** For Everyone Leaving, Let's Order Watermelon.

The other way sentences can work to help students remember information is similar to how acronyms work by taking the first letter of each word in a list and using that letter to be the first letter of the word in a sentence. For example:

- Kingdom, Phylum, Class, Order, Family, Genus, Species: Kind Pat Can Only Find his Gigantic Suitcase.
- Mercury, Venus, Earth, Mars, Jupiter, Saturn, Uranus, Neptune: My Very Energetic Mom Just Serve Us Ninety Pizzas.

Successful students have found this to help them tremendously when they need to remember a series or a list. They can study the list with the sentence and then eventually move to studying the sentence while recalling the list.

Rhyme to Remember

There are times when a simple rhyme that explains the rule or date will help the student. There are many of these rhymes already in use but students may also want to make up their own to make it relevant to the topic they are studying. For example:

- "I" before "E" except after "C" or when sounded like "A" as in neighbor or weigh.
- In fourteen-hundred-and-ninety-two, Columbus sailed the ocean blue.

Overload the Senses

A final way to help improve memory is to overload the senses. What this means is when students have important information to remember for an exam, they should apply the information to as many senses as possible. The more senses they involve in studying the information, the more likely they are to remember it. An example is to create a visualization of the material, link it to a tangible object, and imagine what it smells like. By doing this, students can recall the image, the tangible object, or the smell and will likely recall the information that goes with it.

◇◇◇◇◇◇◇◇◇

CHAPTER 34

IMPROVE VOCABULARY

While in college, students develop their vocabulary to be more professional and educated. Part of this comes from taking classes and learning the terms that go along with their area of study, but successful students can go a little further by taking action to develop their vocabulary even more.

Subscribe to a Word-of-the-Day Email

Since most students are online at least once a day anyway, some students subscribe to a word-of-the-day email so they have easy access to a new word each day. The key to making this work is reading the e-mail and usage examples and then making it a point to use the word at least once each day (more if possible).

This same idea can be used by randomly picking a word out of the dictionary or by getting a word of the day calendar. To make it even more fun and beneficial, the student can challenge roommates and friends to use the word and then talk about how each were able to use the word that day.

Learn Roots, Prefixes, and Suffixes

Much of the English language is based on Greek and Latin roots. Additionally, many words contain prefixes and suffixes that are common to the language. People who understand the meaning of these roots, prefixes, and suffixes can decipher the general meaning of new words without consulting a dictionary. Here are some examples:

Some Greek and Latin roots, prefixes, and suffixes

- Ali: Other. Alias, Alibi.
- Amor: Love, Liking. Amorous, Enamored.
- Dura: Lasting. Duration.
- Man: Hand. Manuel, Manicure.
- Vive: Life. Revive, Vivid.
- Ambi-: Both. Ambidextrous.
- Con-: With. Connected, Conspire.
- Inter-: Between. Interstate.
- Mono-: One. Monologue, Monogamy.
- -Cide: Kill. Suicide.
- -Ectomy: Cut. Appendectomy.

Keep a List of New Words

Students who are serious about learning new words keep a list of new words that they encounter so they can look them up in the dictionary. Some students keep this list in a notebook so they have room to write in the definition as well as examples of usage. This way, they can study these new words and become familiar enough with them to actually use them.

Read

A student must be exposed to a word several times before he or she will be able to remember it and use it properly. This is the reason that the more they read, the more words they will learn. Some students like to read the dictionary when they have time or are taking a break from their studies. They find words and their meanings fascinating. It does not have to be the dictionary, though. Students who read fiction, newspapers, and magazines will also benefit by increasing their vocabulary as well.

Play

Word games such as Scrabble and crossword puzzles challenge the students' vocabularies and force them to learn about new words to succeed at the game.

CHAPTER 35

STAY MOTIVATED

I t is a fact that college is hard work. So hard, in fact, that some students just want to give up and have fun for a while. While taking a night off here and there is not detrimental to a student's college education, doing it consistently may though. Even successful students find they lack motivation to do their schoolwork once and a while. It is how they manage these instances of low motivation that sets them apart from other students.

Examine Lack of Motivation

Successful students first examine the reason they have a lack of motivation for studying. Once they find out why it is there, they will better know how to fix it.

- A lack of motivation due to not being interested in the classes may mean the student needs to reevaluate his or her course of study.

- A lack of motivation because the student does not enjoy a particular class may mean the student decides if he or she needs to be taking the class. If it is not a required class, it may be worth dropping it.

- A lack of motivation resulting from being exhausted may mean the student needs to reorganize his or her schedule or adopt healthier habits.

- A lack of motivation stemming from personal or relationship issues may mean that the student should look into counseling.

Avoid Relying on Other People

An important lesson that most successful students learn early on is they cannot rely on other people to motivate, remind, or force them to get their work done. It does not happen at the college level. Some students, especially first-year students, struggle with the adjustment process of no longer being monitored by their parents. Additionally, college professors don't hound students to get their work done or call them in for meetings if it looks like they are falling behind like high school teachers do. It is up to the student to make the time to study and then actually use that time for effective studying.

Stay Positive and Keep Things in Perspective

Another reason students may lose motivation is if they are so overwhelmed that they feel like nothing they do will make a difference. If they have an extremely tough class that they have been struggling with all semester, they may lose the motivation to put the necessary time into the final exam because they do not feel like they have it in them to learn the material.

What successful students have learned, however, is it is important to put things into perspective. They may want to go out with their friends instead of staying in to study for that last final. They know, though, that if they do not do well on the final, then they may have to retake the class; so they need to decide if one night out is worth retaking an entire class. Plus, they are in college; they know there will be something to do the following night anyway. By putting things into perspective, they can motivate themselves to study when they need to get it done.

Make Lists

Some students work best when they can visualize what they have done and what they have left to do. A great motivator for these people is to write lists. The best way to do this is to write each item as a specific task that is easily identified once it is complete. Once the task is complete, the successful student takes great pride in crossing that item off the list. Seeing the list of things left to do shrink is a great motivator to finish it all. After all, there is no better feeling for list makers than to have a to-do list that is completely empty!

Start Small

Even with all of these great tips, sometimes the most successful students are unable to motivate themselves to do what needs to be done. This is when it is time for students to trick themselves into working. Sometimes it is successful and other times it is not, but at least the student will have accomplished something. Here is how it works:

A successful student may put off starting an assignment for a variety of reasons. She knows she needs to at least get a start on it, but it is her evening to relax. She has about 25 minutes until her favorite television show starts. So, she tells herself she needs to sit down and read through the assignment sheet and make up a plan to complete the assignment sheet before she watches her show. This small task does not sound too bad and she knows if she gets right on task, she can have it done within about 15 minutes. She finds her materials, sits down at that table, and begins reading the assignment sheet.

At this point, one of three things can happen:

- **Situation A.** The student reads through the sheet, jots down questions, and makes a plan. She is done within 15 minutes and has a solid idea of what needs to be done to complete the project. Plus, she knows what she needs to be thinking about to get the project going.

- **Situation B.** The student reads through the sheet, jots down questions, and makes a plan. Then, she realizes she already knows what prompt she wants to use because one popped out at her when she was reading through them. In addition, she initially thought about three possible topics that may work depending on the information available. She looks at the clock and sees she still has ten minutes until her show starts so she gets on the library's online catalog to see what types of information would be available for her possible topics to help her decide. She knows she does not need to make her decision right away, but she has things to think about to get the project moving in her brain.

- **Situation C.** The student reads through the sheet, but as she is doing so, she realizes she does not understand the prompt and how it relates to the course and the topics discussed in class. She writes several questions on the sheet as she reads through it and then double checks her professors office hours to see when she can plan to go ask him or her about the assignment.

Whichever situation occurred, the student accomplished something that night. In situation B, she tricked herself into completing more than she planned. In situation C, she was relieved she had taken the time to read through the assignment sheet so she would have enough time to schedule a meeting with the professor.

CHAPTER 36

MAXIMIZE SUMMER AND SEMESTER BREAKS

The first instinct for most students is to spend their summer and semester breaks relaxing and having fun. While there may be nothing wrong with doing this, successful students like to take advantages of these breaks from taking a full load of credits to both prepare for the upcoming school year as well as to do things that will help them after college. Plus, if they plan it right, they can still have fun and relax for part of the time while making the most of the rest of the time.

Enroll in Summer School

Students who take summer school like this opportunity for many reasons.

- It can help them get ahead and possibly even graduate a semester or even year earlier than if they had not taken summer courses.

- The students could take the classes in the summer and then enroll in a lighter load during the school year while still staying on track to graduate at the normal time. This is especially useful for students who know they will have to take demanding classes in the upcoming year.

- Since summer school sessions are usually shorter in duration (for example, class for 3 hours a day, 4 days a week, for 4 weeks instead of 3 hours a week for 16 weeks), students who are dreading taking a particular class can take it in the summer and get it over with quickly.

Students who are planning on taking summer school should plan carefully, however, because only certain classes are offered in the summer so they should save these classes for summer.

Do an Internship

Students who participate in an internship can spend the summer building their resumes, exploring their proposed career tracks, and even getting an "in" with a company that could possibly hire them in the future. At the very least, they will build up some networking as well as references for when they apply for a job after graduation.

Internships have other benefits as well:

- They help students confirm whether or not they are making the right career and educational choices.

- They give the students valuable insights to take back to the classroom the next year in school.

- They allow the students to make real world connections to what they are learning in the classroom.

- They give the students the motivation they need to successfully finish the last few semesters before graduation.

Volunteer

Many colleges and universities have volunteer programs to help students find organizations to help. Volunteering can be done during the school year, summer, or a semester or spring break. Some universities even offer volunteering vacations instead of the traditional spring break destinations for students.

Volunteering helps students learn more about their area of study, feel good about doing something good for other people, reach one or more of their goals, become more independent, and become more appreciative of everything they have. All in all, volunteering is an invaluable learning experience that students may not have the time to do once they graduate and find themselves holding down a real job.

CHAPTER 37

EASE THE TRANSITION

T ransitioning from high school or full-time employment into a full-time college student can be a difficult transition for many people. The independence, the varied schedules, and the new demands put on each student can often be a difficult adjustment. Learning how to anticipate and fend off these transition issues can make the difference between a student and a successful student.

Anticipate the Learning Style

Extremely successful high school students often have a difficult time transitioning into the new learning style of college. In high school, they thrived on the contact with teachers, a solid schedule, study halls, and the relatively low work load overall. In college, students struggle because they often have to start studying or figure out a new way to study. They also struggle with the concept that no one holds them accountable for what they do or do not do.

Successful students who transition to the new learning style take the time to examine their study methods, learn new study methods, and explore the many resources available to them to help them keep up with their success.

Ease the Fears

While many will not admit it, students often have a difficult time transitioning into college because they fear the unknown. Many have not been away from home before, have thrived on the comfort of their hometown, and the familiarity of their classmates. Venturing to college is a huge step and many students do not know what to expect and are not experienced in things they will now be responsible for such as laundry or cooking. Successful students have found ways to ease these transitions:

- Going to the freshmen orientation meetings is a great help in learning about the university, learning tips for surviving on campus, understanding campus rules and regulations, and meeting new people.

- Looking for freshman transition meetings. These meeting may be held in residence halls, at the union, or in the library. They can cover a myriad of topics such as learning to be in a home away from home (laundry, cleaning, cooking), budgeting, time management, and campus tours.

- Joining a club or organization can help the student meet new people in a social setting right away. This will help them find students who are experiencing the same transition as well as students who have been through it and survived.

Transitioning the Non-traditional Student

Non-traditional students go through a transition process as well. Here are some tips to help them ease into college life:

- Non-traditional students generally do not live in residence halls on campus, so they often feel slightly disconnected from the university as a whole. They can solve this by spending time on campus during the day such as relaxing in the union and studying at the library instead of going home.

- Non-traditional students often have to adjust from working full-time to having a schedule mixed between classes and free time. They often struggle with using this free time if their job was demanding all day long or struggle with attending classes if their job included more independence. They way to solve this problem is to see each day as a workday from 8 a.m. until 5 p.m. and use that time accordingly for studying and classes.

- Non-traditional students sometimes feel alone. They can alleviate this feeling by attending non-traditional student orientation to meet other non-traditional students. They can also join clubs and organizations for their major and minor department. Some universities also offer seminars for adult continuing education that can help non-traditional students overcome their transitioning struggles.

CHAPTER 38

APPROACH THE PROFESSOR

t is highly unlikely that any successful student will graduate from college without approaching a professor outside of class at least once. How they go about meeting with the professor can make or break the professor's opinion of the student. While this section of the book is not advocating sucking up to the professor, it is logical for the student to want the professor on his or her side at all times.

Set up a Meeting

The first thing a student needs to do when trying to meet with a professor is check the professor's office hours. Even though the office hours are there for the professor to meet with students, it is best to try to set something up ahead of time just in case the professor does not already have meetings scheduled with another student. This can be done with an e-mail or phone call to the professor's office.

There will be times when the student has a quick question for the professor and chooses to just stop by during the posted office hours. This is acceptable, but it is best to not drop in during the last few minutes of the schedule office hours. If the professor has to go to a meeting or a class immediately following office hours, he or she will not be able to give his or her full attention to the question.

Prepare for the Meeting

Once the meeting is set, it is important for the student to prepare for the meeting. This includes making a list of questions and gathering all relevant material including class notes and the textbook. The student should also bring a notebook and pen to take notes of the meeting with the professor.

Be Polite

There is nothing worse for a professor than to have a student enter his or her office and be disrespectful, unappreciative, blaming, or otherwise impolite. Successful students realize that professors are people too and they want people to be nice to them. Plus, students who are polite and respectful will be more likely to get a favorable response from the professor, whether they are asking for extra help or even contesting a grade.

Keep Expectations in Check

Students who go to see the professor expecting that they will get exactly what they want when they want it will be sorely disappointed most of the time. Just because a student goes in to contest a grade on an assignment or exam does not mean the professor is going to change that grade, even if the student "knows" they have good reason to request the change. Students should also not expect to get a direct answer from the professor. The professor may make suggestions or give hints towards the answer, but most will want the student to continue thinking about the problem instead of getting a solution handed to them.

Stay Open-Minded

Because some students spend so much time looking at the end point – finishing the paper, acing the exam, completing the semester, and even finally holding that degree in their hands –they start to have tunnel vision and forget there are multiple ways to do things and many viewpoints to consider along the way.

It is not unusual for a student to meet with a professor about a problem, misunderstanding, or a need for guidance with his or her mind set one way. It is the professor's job to help the student look at the issue from other perspectives and if the student cannot widen his or her tunnel vision to see things differently, it is likely the meeting will end without making much progress.

For example, a student may be having difficulties finding information for a research project. They meet with the professor for suggestions and the professor simply says, "Try varying your search terms." To the student, this is no help at all because the answer is not what she was looking for. She wanted some specific locations or search terms to get her started. The professor, however, refuses to give this information to the student because part of the grade for the research paper depends on how well the student can use her resources to find the necessary information. The student then struggles through lists of search terms as one idea leads to another. The student later realizes the value in that lesson because, with practice, researching has become very easy for her.

Successful students attend meetings with professors with an open mind so they can fully listen to and comprehend the suggestions the professor makes to help them, even if the suggestions do not seem helpful at the moment.

CONCLUSION

I t is now time for the student to decide what type of student to be. They can be the student who does nothing but study all the time. They could also be the student who is constantly struggling to keep up and forcing him- or herself to cram the night before exams because he or she has not yet taken the time to get organized and make a plan. If the student wants to get the most out of college, however, he or she is, or is striving to become, the balanced student who knows how to study efficiently so that he or she has time to have fun and participate in activities other than attending class and study sessions.

This book is not the magic wand that will suddenly make studying so easy that the successful student will no longer need to work hard. No book can make a student succeed without his or her own motivation. Instead, this book provides students with the tools needed to become more effective and only they can ensure the tools are put to proper use. Instead, it is my hope that all students who read this book find at least a few nuggets of wisdom to help make their college careers more enjoyable by helping them carve out the time needed to do well in their classes and enjoy the journey.

Happy studying!

BIBLIOGRAPHY

Felder, Richard M., and Barabara A. Soloman. "Learning Styles and Strategies." **www.ncsu.edu**.

Jacobs, Lynn F. and Jeremy S. Hyman. *Professor's Guide to Getting Good Grades in College.* (2006). New York: HarperCollins.

Kingsbury, Alex. "Get in, show up, drop out: Trying to learn why so many college students fail to graduate." *US News & World Report.* November 20, 2005.

Newport, Cal. *How to Become a Straight-A Student: The Unconventional Strategies Real College Students Use to Score High While Studying Less.* (2007). New York: Broadway Books.

Newport, Cal. *How to Win at College: Surprising Secrets for Success from the Country's Top Students.* (2005). New York: Broadway Books.

Pauk, Walter. *How to Study in College 7th Edition.* (2001). New York: Houghton Mifflin.

Reynolds, Jean. *Succeeding in College: Study Skills and Strategies, 2nd Edition* (2002). United States: Prentice Hall.

Van Blerkhom, Dianna L. *College Study Skills: Becoming a Strategic Learner 5th ed.* (2006). United States: Thomson Wadsworth.

ABOUT THE AUTHOR

Susan Roubidoux is a former high school language arts teacher and has also developed study skills workshops for both the high school and collegiate levels. She has a Bachelor of Science, Secondary Education in English and Communication from the University of Wisconsin Oshkosh. She is currently a freelance writer in Winneconne, Wisconsin where she lives with her husband and three sons.

INDEX

A

activities 8-10, 34-40, 221-222

anxiety 124, 137-142, 240-242

appearance 50-52, 206, 257-258

assignments 14-18, 28-40, 29-40, 31-40, 56-64, 65-76, 93-94, 96, 109-110, 114-124, 159-186, 161-186, 187-190, 191-194, 195-198, 199-206, 200-206, 202-206, 209-212, 210-212, 220, 225-230, 244

aural learner 6-10, 59-64

B

backpack 47-52, 256-258

balance 11-12, 30-40, 55-64, 176-186, 223-224

books 3-10, 32-40, 57-64, 65-76, 74-76, 85-94, 97-104, 197-198

brainstorming 191-194, 202-206

breaks 15-18, 21-40, 28-40, 72-76, 79-84, 103-104, 226-230, 252-254, 267-270

C

color-coding 37-40, 49-52

comfort 272-274

comprehension 67-76, 73-76, 82-84, 120-124, 169-186

concentration levels 34-40

critical thinking 16-18, 74-76, 106-110, 151-154, 178-186

D

distractions 16-18, 19-40, 42-46, 48-52, 68-76, 87-94, 135-136, 204-206, 222, 229-230, 252-254

dorm 44, 45, 229

E

email 32-40, 211-212, 215-220, 251-254, 259-262

energy 34-40

essay 39-40, 108-110, 116-124, 126-136, 141-142, 149-150, 151-154, 156-158, 174-186, 227-230

essay questions 126, 134, 152, 156, 227

exams 21-40, 56-64, 75-76, 90-94, 97-104, 108-110, 111-124, 130-136, 143-148, 149-150, 151-154, 155-158, 225-230, 226-230, 279-280

exercise 5-10, 33-40, 44-46, 50-52, 61-64, 79-84, 94, 102-104, 256-258

extracurricular activities 221-222

F

finals 224, 225-230,

flashcards 64, 130-136

freewriting 202-206

G

global learner 6-10, 59-64

grammar 75-76, 120-124, 142, 188-190, 202-206, 255-258

H

highlighters 48-52, 57-64, 88-94

history 37-40, 46, 75-76, 131-136

I

intuitive learner 56-64

J

job 79-84, 185-186, 222, 223-224, 249-250, 268-270, 273-274, 277-278

K

keywords 71-76, 130-136, 162-186, 198

L

lateral thinking 106-110

learning styles 53-64, 161-186,

lectures 14-18, 53-64, 97-104, 117-124, 156-158, 164-186,

library 23-40, 43-46, 59-64, 76, 81-84, 121-124, 136, 195-198, 201-206, 203-206, 239-242, 266, 272-274

M

mistakes 56-64, 91-94, 137-142, 147-148, 155-158, 167-186, 199-206, 213-220, 227-230, 244

N

note-taking 85-94, 99-104, 156-158

O

objective exam 143-148

organize 5-10, 32-40, 47-52, 115-124

P

physical learner 60-64

Q

questions 14-18, 27-40, 51-52, 56-64, 70-76, 78-84, 86-94, 98-104, 107-110, 113-124, 126-136, 138-142, 144-148, 150, 152-154, 156-158, 172-186, 192-194, 197-198, 202-206, 209-212, 227-230, 239-242, 244, 253-254, 266, 276-278

quiet 24-40, 43-46, 48-52, 204-206, 216-220, 253-254

R

reading 4-10, 14-18, 22-40, 54-64, 67-76, 78-84, 87-94, 96, 97-104, 107-110, 114-124, 126-136, 158, 169-186, 189-190, 211-212, 235-242, 253-254, 259-262, 265-266

reflective learning 55-64

research 40, 64, 76, 84, 89-94, 123-124, 136, 162-186, 188-190, 195-198, 196-198, 201-206, 234, 241-242, 277-278

research paper 187-190, 277-278

review sessions 134-136

S

schedule 5-10, 21-40, 104, 115-124, 225-230

science 76, 120-124, 131-136, 283-284

sensing learner 55-64

sequential learner 58-64

signal words 73-76, 99-104

skimming   72-76, 103-104, 107-110

snack   27-40, 101-104, 252-254,

social media   28-40

solving problems   55-64

sources   56-64, 83-84, 164-186, 188-190, 192-194, 195-198, 206

spelling   142, 202-206

SQ3R method   79, 82, 83

stress   22-40, 48-52, 57-64, 65-76, 104, 134-136, 192-194, 225-230, 226-230

student union   23-40, 121-124

study blocks   27-40

study groups   50-52, 58-64, 62-64, 122-124, 133-136, 134-136

study spot   24-40, 42-46

T

technology   207-212, 241-242

thesis   150, 197-198, 200-206

timelines   57-64, 132-136, 189-190

time management   21-40, 47-52, 240-242

U

underlining   85

V

verbal learner   57-64

vertical thinking   107-110, 108-110

visual depictions   132-136, 203-206

visual learner   57-64

vocabulary   68-76, 75-76, 98-104, 120-124, 259-262

W

writing   22-40, 58-64, 68-76, 85-94, 99-104, 109-110, 121-124, 138-142, 149-150, 153-154, 183-186, 192-194, 197-198, 199-206, 207-212, 235-242, 244